## CELEBRATION OF HAND-HOOKED RUGS 32

### 2022 Edition

Editor
Mark Allison

Coordinator
Caitlin Eaton

Graphic Designer
Matt Paulson

Advertising Coordinator
Chris Wright

Customer Service
Ampry Publishing, LLC
rughook@amprycp.com

Publisher
Ampry Publishing, LLC

Rug photographs provided by the artists unless otherwise noted.

*Rug Hooking* (ISSN 1045-4373) is published five times a year in Jan./Feb., March/April/May, June/July/Aug.,Sept./Oct., and Nov./Dec. by Ampry Publishing, LLC, 3400 Dundee Road, Suite 220, Northbrook, IL 60062.

A Publication of

# R·U·G HOOKING

P.O. Box 490
New Cumberland, PA  17070

www.rughookingmagazine.com
rughook@amprycp.com

ISBN 978-1-945550-61-4
Printed in U.S.A.

# WELCOME TO C

## *Honoring the Spirit of Creativity in the Rug Hooking Community*

The 32nd edition of this annual publication is cause for celebration!

Not only does this publication celebrate the talent, hard work, and inspiration of the 64 artists whose handiwork is featured in these pages, it is a testament to the indefatigable spirit of creativity that flourishes in the rug hooking community. To say that the past few years have been challenging for just about everyone is something of an understatement. That's why it's such a pleasure to be able to share these wonderful examples of the power of imagination and inventiveness. It's a way of recognizing the work of top-notch artists, both in the U.S. and abroad, and to inspire our readers to pursue their own artistic endeavors in the face of challenges big and small.

I'd like to make special note of the incredible variety of rugs featured this year. They range from lively, whimsical, and joyous to peaceful, wistful, and poignant; from bold, graphic, and representational to subtle, understated, and impressionistic. Taken together, they exemplify the impressive ambition and reach of our community, from beginner to expert and everyone in between.

And it's not just the featured rugs that have provided a much-appreciated boost of inspiration. Each of the artworks submitted for consideration has inspired us, demonstrating in no uncertain terms that the imaginative spirit is persistent and powerful. Creativity breeds creativity. In the words of Maya Angelou: "You can't use up creativity. The more you use, the more you have."

Mark Allison
*Rug Hooking* Magazine Editor

**ON THE COVER:** *Black and White*, hooked by Tatiana Knodel. Turn to page 10 to learn more about this rug.

# Table of Contents

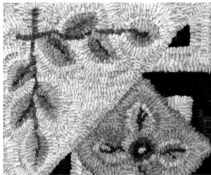

## RUGS BASED ON ADAPTATIONS

# Meet the Judges

Each year, our judges take on a mountain of a task. With nearly 200 entries, each containing four separate photos, the judges patiently spend many hours reviewing and evaluating each rug. While the convenience of an online system allows the judges to peruse the entries at their own pace from the comfort of their favorite chair, surrounded by snacks of their choice, it's still a job that takes an incredible amount of time and energy. We're so grateful to our judges for their many hours of deliberation and careful consideration, all in the name of rug hooking. Their expertise and experience is invaluable. And so, we'd like to extend our thanks to these four judges, along with all the judges who have gone before them.

## Stephanie Allen-Krauss

Stephanie Allen-Krauss is a fourth-generation rug hooker who learned rug hooking at age six from her mother, Anne Ashworth, a nationally-known rug hooking teacher. During her teenage years, her mother taught her about dyeing and later about repairing rugs. In 1999 she opened a retail shop in Montpelier, Vermont, Green Mountain Hooked Rugs, where she sells supplies for rug hookers, teach classes and offer rug repair. In 2010, she was awarded the Governor's Heritage Award for Outstanding Traditional Artist in the state of Vermont. Her rugs have received numerous awards and have been featured in several national publications. To date, her body of work includes more than 300 hooked rugs.

She has been the director of two rug hooking schools: Green Mountain Rug School and Fall Fiesta Rug School. Most recently she's enjoyed an exploration of antique geometric rugs; she is the lead restorer for a large private collection of antique hooked rugs. Seven rugs of her original designs are now in this private collection as well. She lives in Montpelier, Vermont, with her ever-patient husband and their aging cat.

## Rachelle LeBlanc

Rachelle LeBlanc's work is renowned worldwide for its distinct style and technical prowess. In 2012, she was awarded the Alberta Creative Development Initiative Grant to Individuals from the Canada Council for the Arts and the Alberta Foundation for the Arts. She has work in the Alberta Foundations of the Arts and the Royal Alberta Museum permanent collections. Her work has been exhibited in galleries in Canada and the United States, including the Robert Bateman Foundation Gallery, Art Gallery of Alberta, Harbourfront Center, Yeiser Art Center, Lawndale multidisciplinary contemporary art center, and The Gallery at the University of Connecticut. She teaches workshops throughout Canada and the US, and currently lives in Katy, Texas.

## Pris Buttler

Pris Buttler is an artist with many years of experience in the art world, first as a graphic designer and then rug hooking teacher, along with oil painting. She was on the national circuit of teaching this wonderful art form of rug hooking and taught in many areas of the U.S. and Canada. She holds a graphic design degree from Pikes Peak Community College in Colorado Springs, Colorado. She worked for Current Greeting Cards in Colorado, owned and ran her own design business in Gainesville, Georgia, was a freelance graphic designer for many companies nationwide, and has extensive training as a folk and fine artist, studying with many well-known art teachers in all subjects of representational oil painting. Presently her field of interest is in portraiture and figurative paintings.

## Sara Judith

Sara Judith had been teaching rug hooking since 1999. She recently retired to, as she says, spend the rest of her time in this world as a painter. Over the years she has been featured in *Rug Hooking* magazine, *Celebration VIII* and *X*, Anne Mather's book, *Creative Rug Hooking*, in which she wrote a chapter on lettering for the rug hooker. She also has a chapter in Jessie Turbayne's book, *Hooked Rugs of the Deep South*. *Rug Hooking* magazine featured her rugs inspired by the painter Gustav Klimt. Over the years she has taught in many rug hooking schools and workshops and enjoys the wonderful world of women who love each other and their art. She wrote three dye books, a catalog with more than 125 pattern designs, and two instruction booklets: "Easy Lettering Tips for the Rug Hooker" and "Basic Design for the Rug Hooker."

# Spread the Joy of Rug Hooking and Punch Needle!

If you're interested in learning rug hooking or punch needle, or if you want to share the art form with a friend or family member, then try our popular introductory books!

*Introduction to Rug Hooking: A Beginner's Guide to Tools, Techniques, & Materials* guides you though the basic techniques that every rug hooker needs to know. Plus, it includes eight step-by-step projects.

*Mastering the Art of Punch Needle Rug Hooking: Techniques and Projects* leads you through the basics of starting your punch journey. Find detailed instructions for beginner and experienced punchers, plus six projects.

**Order online:**
**www.rughookingmagazine.com/STORE**

# HALCYON

MAINE YARN EST. 1971

HALCYONYARN.COM • 800.341.0282 • 12 SCHOOL STREET • BATH, MAINE

*Shop our complete selection online, and sign up for our email newsletter so you never miss a deal!*

Halcyon Yarn is your source for inspiration, great service, and selection. Hundreds of yarns, fibers, and tools in stock. From books and hooks, to dyes, backings, frames and Classic Rug Wool yarns. Halcyon's Classic Rug Wools are available in three weights and over 100 colors, plus 46" single strands for accent work.

# *Awakening*

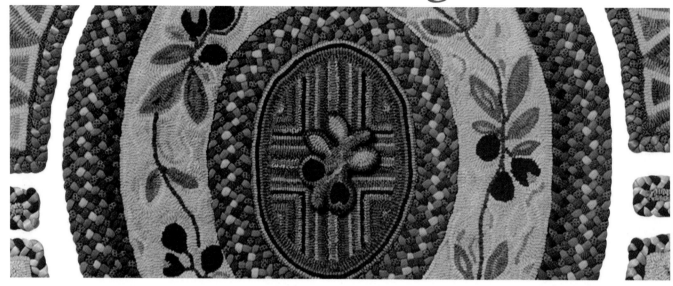

I got the idea of the lychee nuts from a platter I bought at the Brattleboro Area Hospice's shop shop, Experienced Goods, in Brattleboro, Vermont. I loved the cranberry-colored nuts and the greens of the leaves. After hooking and braiding the center I realized I would never walk on it, so I decided to make it for the wall. Due to the weight of the braids, I made it in multiple pieces and let my wall become part of the finished piece. There would be about 1½″ of air space between each piece, with the wall considered just as important as the hooked and braided sections. The project grew to 10 sections, using the common theme of simple leaves and nuts throughout.

At the time I was working on the sections, I took a class in joomchi* felting and decided to combine the joomchi and the hooked and braided sections using the common leaf pattern as a base. I had wanted to backlight one of my fiber art creations; my brother, Tim Mathiesen, is a wonderful lighting designer.

*Awakening* was taking shape over the winter of 2021 during the pandemic and stay-at-home orders. Tim began looking at how best to light the joomchi elements. After exploring how natural backlighting enhanced the wonderful qualities of the handmade paper, we settled on using a light box. The shallow depth of the box would contain a sheet of LEDs, with layers of diffusion to help soften or smooth the light.

My husband, Stewart, built the lightbox and we three figured out how to attach the three layers of joomchi felting. The LEDs are tunable white (they can be a warm, neutral, or cool white depending on the room setting), and we used a dimmer to have ultimate control of the lighting effect.

The lights make the felting shine and brought out the color of the wool and silk used in the hooking and braiding. The piece needs the natural light (or overhead display lights) of the room, plus the brilliance of the back-lit joomchi.

I love the texture that silk and wool bring to my art: the silk shines, the wool is cool, and together they dance.

Be open to changes in life and in making art!

*\* Joomchi is a "centuries-old Korean paper-making technique that uses water to seal several layers of thin, handmade mulberry papers together to form a single, strong sheet. The paper is first wetted, then aggressively gripped, grabbed, stretched, and manipulated until the fibers are broken down, or felted. A major transformation occurs: flat sheets of paper become a very organic, leather-like, almost living form."—Susan Avishai*

### Kris McDermet
Dummerston, Vermont

*Kris McDermet learned to braid and hook during the same year (1979) and experimented with combination pieces early on. Hooking and braiding complement each other and neither has more importance in this piece. Teaching "After the Hooking Comes Braiding" and meeting new people and passing on the art/craft of braiding and hooking are my great loves.*

**In The Judges' Eyes:** *Beautiful use of braiding in conjunction with hooking. Stunning use of color; a true work of art. Exquisite braided finish.*

**Awakening**, 53″ x 70″, #5-, 6-, 7-cut hand-dyed wool and silk on linen.
Joomchi fabricated from mulberry paper with wool and silk fibers, and backlit with LED lights.
Designed, hooked, and braided by Kris McDermet, Dummerston, Vermont, 2021.
Lighting by Tim Mathiesen, West Brattleboro, Vermont, 2021.

# Black and White

Geometric design has always appealed to me because I have made a lot of engineering drawings in my life. This is the way my mind works, and I understand geometrics, repeats, straight lines, and how units work together. My intention was to create a 3-D illusion without using a sculpting technique.

Usually I do not color plan the entire rug before I begin to hook it. But in the case of this rug, I chose the colors first. The black and white wools were the obvious choices. For the background color, I hooked bittersweet swatches. The black and white are very bright, so for the background I needed some muted tone color.

I enjoyed hooking all sections of the rug. The motifs were all challenging.

I used my own technique of hooking straight lines, which I developed when I hooked the rug *Flying Geese*. To make the lines straight, I first hooked the lines in the usual way, then I shaped the last line with scissors. The scissors must be sharp and should be held vertically. I only cut those loops that are not right on the straight line. I use this technique for almost all the lines in my rugs, even if they are not straight lines. When I do this, everything will have a well-defined outer contour. This technique works well for cuts #3 and #4. This was the perfect rug to perfect my technique for hooking straight lines.

I whipped the edges of the rug with wool yarn in such a way that the yarn can hardly be seen, and I finished the rug with binding tape.

**Tatiana Knodel**
Sudbury, Ontario

*Tatiana Knodel began rug hooking in 2008. She has made more than 180 hooked pieces. Tatiana's favorite style of rug hooking is a fine cut (#3 and #2) with sculpting. She enjoys all other styles, especially making bags to match clothing.*

**In The Judges' Eyes:** *Difficult shapes hooked well. Intriguing design. Very accurate hooking of geometric lines and shapes.*

**Black and White**, 31½″ x 31½″, #3-cut wool on rug warp.
Designed and hooked by Tatiana Knodel, Sudbury, Ontario, 2020.

# Cherry Blossoms

I have long admired the hooking of April DeConick, and I wondered how using her color theory to hook flowers would work. Having experimented with a few small trivets, I decided to try a larger rug.

Each flower used three different-colored swatches, and I hooked randomly, creating splotches of color rather than hooking in straight lines. Each petal had four value areas; these I drew on each petal, and I hooked a value area using all three colors. The effect was impressionistic rather than realistic— quite a pleasing result. I called what I was doing "non-traditional shading" for want of a better description. I followed petal theory of A, B, and C petals using this non-traditional approach.

The background is unexpected. It was hooked with two soft-colored textured wools that provided a nice contrast to the brighter, dyed wool of the flowers. I thought a geometric design in the background would be interesting and chose a very old Japanese geometric called the key pattern. Probably the most challenging aspect was drawing the geometric design on the diagonal. Thank goodness for different-colored markers, which I used when I needed to make corrections.

I enjoyed hooking the flowers the most; it was fun choosing the colors to work with and experimenting with this non-traditional shading. I love shading.

I finished the rug by turning the linen forward and whipping.

My main lesson from this rug is that trying a new approach or technique is always a learning experience that stretches you. Try something new—you might just like it!

**Susan Grant**
Acton, Ontario

*Susan Grant is a member of the Georgetown Rug Hooking Guild and the Ontario Hooking Craft Guild. She is also a member of the* Celebration *Hall of Fame, having had seven rugs in* Celebration.

**In The Judges' Eyes:** *The flowers are creatively and beautifully shaded. The geometric background is perfectly executed. Superior rug! Love the way you hooked the flower petals.*

**Cherry Blossoms**, 36″ x 55″, #4-, 5-, 6-, and 8-cut hand-dyed and as-is wool, and banana silk yarn on linen.
Designed and hooked by Susan Grant, Acton, Ontario, 2021.

# Dancing Prism

In my first attempt at hooking a geometric pattern, I wanted to create movement from a static design. The major source of this movement was achieved by using dip dyes; hooking from light to dark, then dark to light; and finally by using the same light-to-dark element for each of the different colors across the rug. The colors moved from pink, bright pink, and purple, to purple, green, blue, and violet. This brought all the separate color rows together, moving as one—light to dark, and back again.

The center accented shapes are a steady area, a place for your eye to rest. They also alternate their colors top to bottom, remaining consistent diagonally.

I love this background. It adds a subtle diagonal movement, like a wave passing beneath the pattern above. The neutral wool used in the background also transitions from light to dark, dark to light. The lightest is a silver-flecked wool, followed by a gold-flecked wool, a light textured neutral, and a heavier textured for the darkest. Your eye dances along this rug, not wanting to stop.

**Pam Manders**
Arnold, Maryland

*Pam Manders has been hooking since 2007 and is very active in her local McGown guild. Her rug hooking career began 15 years ago with a #3-cut pansy pattern.*

**In The Judges' Eyes:** *Gorgeous rendering of the colors, well done! Smooth color transitions and precise hooking make for a pleasing effect. Great use of color.*

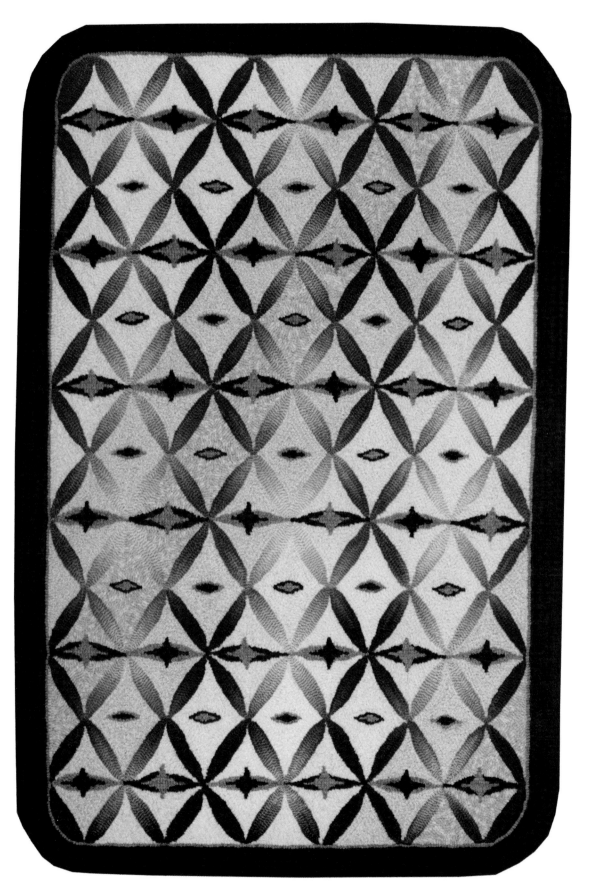

**Dancing Prism**, 26″ x 40″, #3-, 4-, 5-cut hand dyed and as is wool on rug warp.
Designed and hooked by Pam Manders, Arnold, Maryland, 2021.

# Fire Season

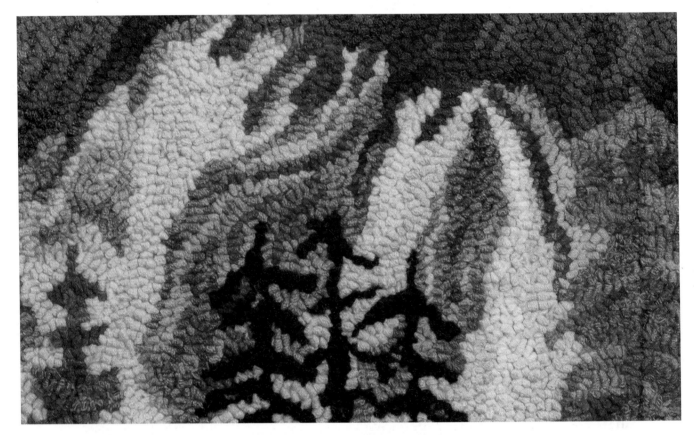

I started *Fire Season* late in the summer of 2019. At the time the West was being ravaged by wildfires. 2019 was a bad fire season for the West, and the destruction was repeated in 2020 and 2021 with equal ferocity. In all three years, the smoke extended completely across the U.S. and Canada, all the way to the East Coast. For days on end, we here in Oregon never saw the sky, and the sun only appeared as an eerie, dirty, orange glow. I live in a rural area near the USFS Redmond Fire Aerial Command Center. Aerial tankers flew over our house constantly in the daylight hours all three years. The nonstop flights simply magnified my awareness of how bad the last three fire seasons have been.

Dyeing the wool for the smoke was the challenge. After several attempts, I settled on dyeing the wool in a painting style after it was hooked. Because the dye often bled into the adjacent wool, I had to go back and re-hooked the "non-smokey" areas. I really think the smoke is the best part of the rug. I wanted to create the illusion of spontaneous combustion in the tall trees. It certainly was a challenge. I think portraying it really added to feeling the intensity and rapid movement of the fire, the intensity of the rug images.

I thought hooking fire would be easy, but it is very complex to pull it off right. Placing yellows where it is the hottest and orange/reds as it cools; using black smoke to indicate a rapidly moving fire—these elements and more had to be placed correctly to be as realistic as possible.

Watching the demonstrators at the country fair inspired me year after year until finally I went to their local meetings.

**Barb Powell**
Redmond, Oregon

*Barb Powell works at being retired by keeping busy with her love of the outdoors. Summers are quite busy with hiking in the Three Sisters Wilderness and camping in the trailer. She belongs to the Tillamook hooking group and the Prairie Harvest Guild.*

**In The Judges' Eyes:** *Vivid color adds to this dramatic scene. Fire and smoke very believably rendered. What a dramatic rug!*

OWEN CAREY

**Fire Season**, 32″x 26″, #3-cut hand-dyed wool on monk's cloth.
Designed and hooked by Barb Powell, Redmond, Oregon, 2021.

# Flying on a Cloudy Day

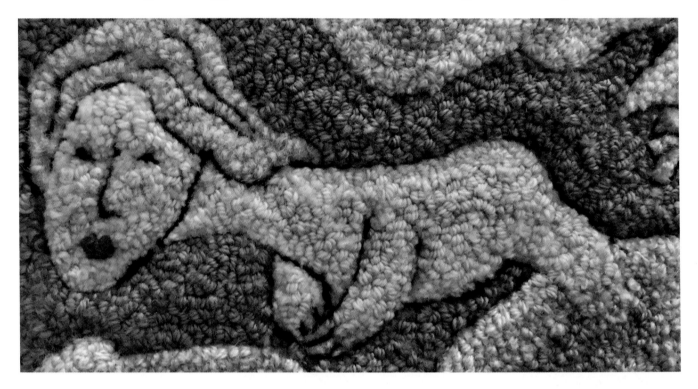

I am enjoying hooking with wool yarn. I can work with long strands. Wool yarn dyes well and easily. And there are so many commercial options. I can buy large bags of yarn at my local thrift store for not much money. And when I get lucky, I find a good amount of usable wool yarn. I donate the yarns I don't use to my local community center fabric arts program.

I think using yarn enhances my designs by allowing me to place my loops close together. This helps create the shading effects I like. In this current series of yarn rugs, I use black yarn to define my edges. I also like the effect I get by of cutting the tops of loops and exposing the darker color tone in the middle of the yarn strand.

The spirals I created in this piece are my favorite elements. The eyes of the two figures on the right are spirals. And starting at the point where the pink figure emerges from the dark area of the cloud, your eye travels in a spiral that ends at the cloud at the top.

Each area of this piece presents its own challenges. For a large single area, I worry that I will run out of that yarn color. If it is a small area, like an eye, defining the parts usually requires more than one try. Color choices are always challenging for me.

This piece has more colors than I generally use. I am kind of amazed at some of my successful color choices. It gives me more confidence to step out of my color comfort zone.

I am new to fabric arts with rug hooking, though I have been a visual artist for a long time. My main media are drawing, painting, and collage. I am looking forward to experimenting with designing a rug from one of my collages.

### Ellie Portner
Sonoma, California

*Ellie Portner loves creating art, music, and poetry. She learned to hook right after she saw a rug show. She had no idea how the art was created but knew immediately that she wanted to learn to do it.*

**In The Judges' Eyes:** *A fun piece, a great design. I absolutely love this one, kudos to the artist. Totally original and such good use of hooking.*

**Flying on a Cloudy Day**, 11″ x 14″, commercial and hand-dyed yarn on monk's cloth.
Designed and hooked by Ellie Portner, Sonoma, California, 2020.

# *Geisha in the Rain*

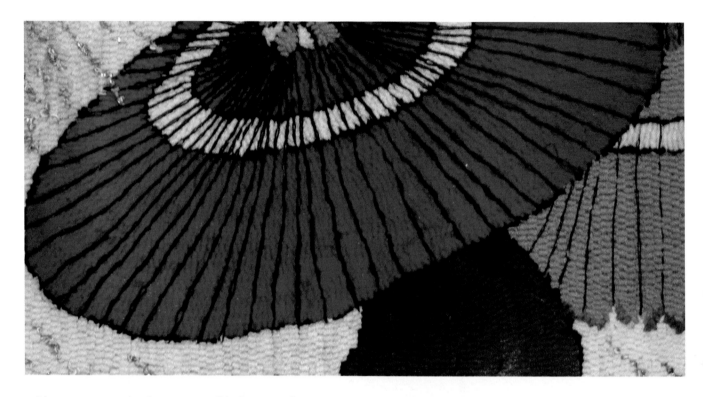

I became interested in Japanese woodblock prints a few years ago after seeing some images online. I began to save the images and research the history and the art styles behind them. One artist, Ohara Koson, really appealed to me—I love the way he depicted flowers and birds, and I'm drawn to his choice of color washes. He also did several so-called "Beauty" prints, showing the famous geishas of the "floating world." This rug is inspired by a detail of one of his prints.

I usually hook with wool fabric on a linen backing, and for the most part, that is how this rug has been done. However, to achieve the slanting rain, I used some metallic yarn that I had in my stash, and I embroidered the spokes on the parasols with embroidery floss.

The best part of the rug, for me, is the kimono, as the colors of the fabric flow and transition in a really natural way. I used a dip-dyed piece of wool for this area, and I had a lot of fun dyeing the wool outside at my cottage this past summer.

The parasols were the biggest challenge, as it proved too difficult to hook the lines of the spokes. I wound up embroidering them overtop of the hooked fabric.

I commissioned my son to make a stretcher frame, and I stretched the backing on this frame, stapling the excess linen to the back, and mitering the corners. I glued ¾" grosgrain ribbon along the outer edge of the frame to give it a more polished look.

I started rug hooking about 30 years ago, with my first (as yet unfinished!) piece intended to be a rug for my eldest son's nursery. I still haven't finished that one, but I really fell in love with the craft and have continued to hook since then. Lately, I've been exploring the possibilities offered by plarn—plastic yarn created by recycling bags. I'm hooking, knitting, and crocheting with it, using the recycling aspect to draw attention to environmental issues facing our environment.

**Caroline M. Simpson**
Fredericton, New Brunswick

*Caroline M. Simpson is a fiber artist working mostly in contemporary rug hooking. She is a juried member of Craft NB and belongs to several hooking guilds. Her work has been exhibited in several galleries in the Maritimes.*

**In The Judges' Eyes:** *Cohesive background colors give a sense of rainy day. The red umbrella adds such interest to this piece. Interpretation is wonderful.*

**Geisha in the Rain**, 13″ x 20″, #5-cut hand-dyed wool and fantasy-fiber yarn on linen.
Designed and hooked by Caroline M. Simpson, Fredericton, New Brunswick, 2021.

# Golden Gate Sunset

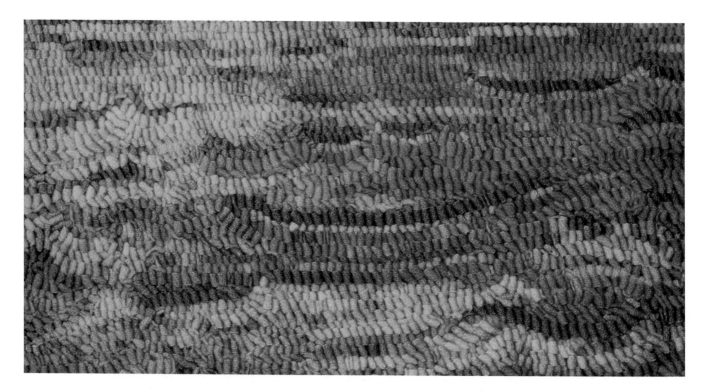

Anticipating a guild workshop called "Wonderscapes" with Brigitta Phy, I looked through my landscape photographs. Living in the San Francisco Bay area, I have many photographs of the Golden Gate Bridge. It's a famous landmark that you can see from many different angles and places around the bay. This rug is based on a photograph taken from a Golden Gate Transit ferry.

The workshop was postponed due to COVID-19, so I left this pattern as a normal landscape. I was involved in a Zoom Rainbow Challenge around this same time and thought I could have the sunset evolve into a kaleidoscopic rainbow sky, with the feeling of a wonderscape. The high clouds above the bay suggested the angle of the parallelograms.

I like to use leftover wool; having to make-do and combining bits can create a rich palette. Often the leftovers from one project go on to the next project. The sky is made up of leftover rainbow swatches; I tried to create a sunset in warm colors and a coming dusk in cool colors. I dyed two transitional spots for the bay waters: For the bright waters, the transition was orange-yellow-green. For the dark waters, the transition was green-blue-purple.

I love the light in this piece, and the movement of the waves. I knew that my water did not have enough contrast, so I had to add some darker strips here and there, and a few more bright wave edges. I had decided that I wouldn't use any green in the sky, but when the rug was completely hooked and finished, it needed a bit of green reflected from the green bay waters. Fortunately, there was a hot magenta parallelogram that was spoiling the effect and needed to come out . . . so the green went in.

A lesson learned from this rug: Pink and magenta are hard to blend with other colors. A lesson reinforced: Contrast is good.

**Laura Pierce**
Petaluma, California

*Laura Pierce has been hooking since 1996. She started teaching in 2003. Laura was inducted into the* Celebration *Hall of Fame in 2018.*

**In The Judges' Eyes:** *The geometric sky is a fabulous twist on a beautiful scene. Wonderful use of pastel palette. Unexpected sky adds sparkle.*

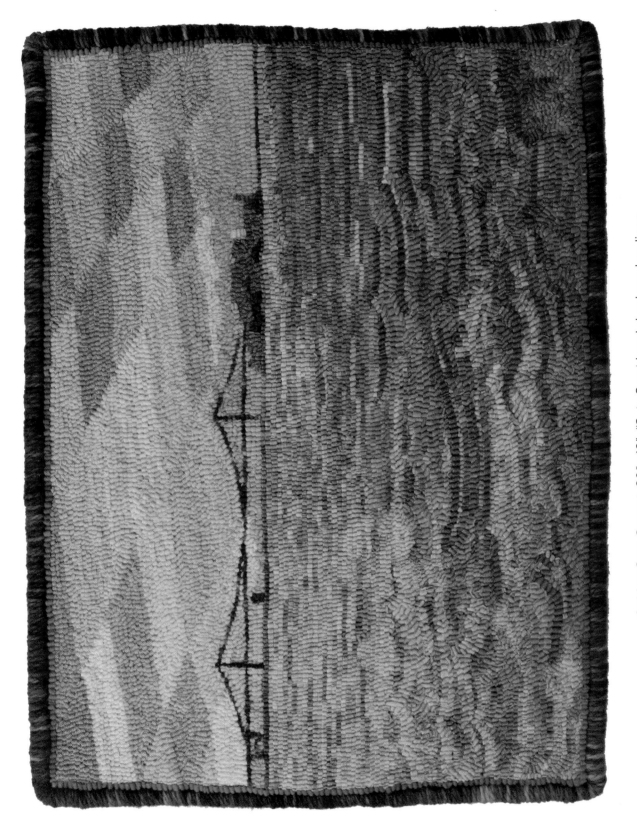

**Golden Gate Sunset,** 20" x 16", #3- to 8-cut hand-dyed wool on linen. Designed and hooked by Laura Pierce, Petaluma, California, 2021.

# Gracie

*Gracie* is a crewel design, using techniques such as antigodlin, pixilating, and 3-cut snips. I wanted to design and hook a bright rug to use interesting techniques.

We created a new technique for the background that we call linen. It consists of using horizontal and vertical lines to create visual contrast with the curved flowers and leaves.

All dyed wool was formulated for this rug using a mixture of both textures and naturals to create interest. The bold colors create a huge contrast with the dark teal background. I aimed to use hot colors in harmony, so that they move through the rug without taking center focus.

The balls of the tassels are done in a Waldoboro technique; the pods are done that way as well, to create harmony throughout the rug.

If using creative stitches on long hooked rugs, be sure to pay attention to the placement of the creative stitches to create movement throughout the piece.

**Anne Bond**
Northville, Michigan

*Anne Bond started hooking rugs, designing patterns, and dyeing wool in 2001. She studied at The Society of Creative Studies in Detroit, Michigan.*

**In The Judges' Eyes:** *The implied lattice in the background is clever. Special techniques add extra interest. Great sculptured knots.*

**Gracie**, 23″ x 65″, #4-, 5-, and 6-cut wool on linen.
Designed and hooked by Anne Bond, Northville, Michigan, 2020.

# Grampa's Pleasure

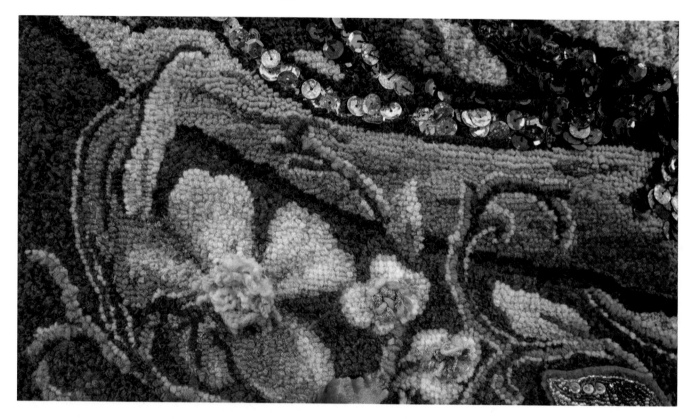

This memory rug honors Grampa doing what he loved, showing him when he was most happy—training his best friend, an English Setter named Ginger. He loved combing the New England fields looking for pheasant.

I added sequins to the feathers, as their rounded shape and sparkle most closely resembled feathers. I hooked novelty yarns in the centers of the flowers and the added beads shine like a wet leaf in the sun. I used many sausage-dyed swatches for the petals and leaves and found a perfect piece of velvet to appliqué.

The pheasant is a strong focal point. I wanted it to look tranquil, not afraid (as they often do in so many hunting pictures). I want my work to transmit an emotion through happy colors and a design that leaves the viewer with a pleasant feeling.

I changed the natural colors of the pheasant (mainly brown) to wild pinks and yellows, to strengthen the focal point. The warm, wild colors stand out from the cool, contrasting border colors.

I whipstitched the edges with cashmere yarn, then I covered a stretched canvas with fabric and sewed the hooking to it.

I learned that reading art books on composition and color planning really are enormously helpful. This was my first time to try sausage dyeing, which I learned from a Zoom class by Linda Powell through the Ontario guild. I will be employing that technique for all my future rugs.

### Grace Collette
Raymond, New Hampshire

*Grace Collette has been included in* Celebration *eight times. She was a featured artist, best of show, people's choice at several Rug Hooking weeks at Sauder Village. She has published articles, won juried membership in the League of NH Craftsmen, and is a member of the* Celebration *Hall of Fame.*

**In The Judges' Eyes:** *Bright colors that make this joyful. Mixed media is a creative choice that enhances the whole piece. Love the background scene!*

**Grampa's Pleasure**, 30″ x 24″, #3-and 8-cut wool and velvet, sequins, beads, and novelty yarns on linen. Designed and hooked by Grace Collette, Raymond, New Hampshire, 2021.

# I Am Cat—Hear Me Mroww

My daughter's very active Japanese bobtail cat, Smudgie, was the inspiration for this hooking. She is the subject of lots of photos; many of them are close-ups because she absolutely loves being right up in your face, meowing in her very distinct voice about whatever is concerning her at that moment. One day a photo stood out from all the rest. I don't know whether it was the expression in her eyes, the angle of her head or what, but I knew I had to hook it.

A problem immediately presented itself. Smudgie is a calico with lots of orange and gold fur, and I've always found it difficult to find the right shades of wool to hook gold-toned animals accurately. In my stash there was absolutely no orange or blond shades of wool until a wonderful woman who was retiring from rug hooking asked me to find a home for her wool. In that inherited wool I found quite a few small bits and pieces of wool in a variety of orange, gold, and yellow tones that—I hoped—together would be enough to hook the cat's orange patches.

Happily, the variety of wool bits was enough. When it was hooked in the direction the fur grows, it made a more realistic version of orange fur patches than if I had dyed or bought larger pieces of wool in fewer shades specifically for this project.

The cat's eyes turned out as I hoped—they really stare at the viewer just as Smudgie herself does. I think her whiskers and ears reaching beyond the edges of the hooking make the portrait more intimate, as though she really is up in your face. Her nose, with its smudges of black and gray, had to be accurate because that is the reason for her name. The snout and cute little cheeks were mottled using a very pale gray. The black in this hooking is not black at all—it is navy blue. I find navy to be sharper than black.

To finish the hooking, I zigzagged the edges as usual, ironed them back, and hand-stitched rug binding over them. Later, when I decided to display this hooking on my family-room wall with other pet portraits, I mounted it on 16" x 16" black stretched canvas.

My method of attaching a hooked piece to a canvas does absolutely no harm to the hooking. No glue needed. Using an upholstery needle threaded with yarn (any color will do because it is invisible on the front of the hooking), I pull the yarn from the back of the canvas through both the canvas and hooked piece and tthen—a few loops away—back through both layers to the back. I pull the yarn just tight enough for it to disappear between loops, and tie a small knot on the back of the canvas. Knots are tied in several places, spaced to support the weight of the hooking. If I need to remove a hooking from a canvas, I only need to clip the yarn and it comes right out. I find this to be a very striking way to display multiple hookings as a group.

**Carol Koerner**
Bethesda, Maryland

*Carol Koerner began rug hooking in 1996 when she was introduced to the artistic rug hooking of Roslyn Logsdon; she has participated in numerous exhibits, winning sseveral awards, including best in show and readers' choice. She has written articles for* Rug Hooking *magazine and ATHA. Other interests are her dog, and judging fine arts at her county fair. Carol is a member of the 2018 class of the* Celebration *Hall of Fame. This is her fifteenth rug in* Celebration.

**In The Judges' Eyes:** *Very lifelike! Well drawn and well hooked. Great eyes!*

**I Am Cat—Hear Me Mroww**, 14″ x 14″, #3-cut wool on linen.
Designed and hooked by Carol Koerner, Bethesda, Maryland, 2020.

# Lockdown Pomegranates & Figs

I moved to England from Northern Virginia during the start of the pandemic. Before my move, I was working on two rugs that I brought in my suitcases, but once I got settled in my new house, I realized I just couldn't work on either of them. Too much thinking was involved! My new old house has 400 year-old brick tile floors that cried out for runners.

January of 2021 was bleak in England; The country was in complete lockdown, and it was raining every day. I had terrible insomnia that couldn't be cured by any number of sessions of Yoga With Adriene.

One night I got up and decided I was going to make a pomegranate fruit runner for the floor, and that it needed to be an old-fashioned rug with a modern feel. I laid out paper and paints and started that night. I cut out giant pomegranates that I shifted around until I liked the design.

Even drawing the cartoon was difficult, as I could only find the thinnest white paper to draw on; I ended up destroying it when I pulled it off the mesh. I didn't even have enough linen, but I managed to piece together the remnants I had since I couldn't bear to wait for a shipment from the United States. I had to do it immediately.

Pomegranates are a favorite of mine—they are symbols of both life and death. I included figs because I like them too, and there is a giant fig tree outside my studio door.

This has been the only rug I have ever made that was designed for a particular spot.

**Barbara Prentice**
Bedfordshire, England

*Barbara Prentice has lived in many places during her husband's naval and civilian careers, both in the United States and overseas. She now lives in England.*

**In The Judges' Eyes:** *Amazing, vibrant, soft colors. Good technique for blending a variety of values. Superb mastery of color, unusual border adds interest.*

**Lockdown Pomegranates and Figs**, 32″ x 72″, #4- and 6-cut hand-dyed wool on linen.
Designed and hooked by Barbara Prentice, Bedfordshire, England, 2021.

# Not So Fishy Stitches

A free online Zoom class called Fishy Stitches was being offered by ATHA Region 11 to learn how to do special or fancy stitches to enhance your rug hooking techniques. It had been several years since I had taken a special stitches class so I decided, since I was stuck at home anyway, that I should give it a try. I wasn't keen on doing a tropical fish, as I live in landlocked Alberta, Canada, and asked Barb if I could do another creature; she agreed. I decided to stay with a water theme and chose a seagull on a sandy beach, with water and sky behind.

I like the traditional look of wool so decided to use more traditional materials.

I love how the sky turned out. And I was pleased with the way the brick-like areas interact with the swirly movement on the opposite side. It makes me feel that the sky is in motion, brewing something and causing the rough, choppy water. Maybe a storm is coming in, or maybe it's just a windy day—it is up to the viewer to decide.

Doing the seagull itself was challenging. I wasn't looking for photorealism, but I wanted the bird to be recognizable as a seagull and have wings and feathers. I dyed up six values of gray and tried to hook my strips to give some depth to the bird. By using directional hooking and a variety of special stitches, I captured the body shape and gave the illusion of feathers.

I whipped the edges with hand-dyed wool yarn, using a herringbone stitch.

Lessons from this rug: Patience, and counting stitches matters!

I started hooking over 20 years ago when I saw a lady working on a small fine-shaded piece while on a horseback riding trip in Saskatchewan. Although I was familiar with hand-hooked rugs, I was not sure how they were crafted. We sat around the campfire after a ride and she showed me what she was doing. I thought, what a great craft! You can do it anywhere! She then introduced me to the Edmonton Rug Hooking Guild, and I was hooked. We are still friends and we both still hook rugs.

**Laurie Wiles**
Edmonton, Alberta

*Laurie Wiles lives and hooks in Edmonton, Alberta. During COVID-19 she has been staying in touch with many of her hooking friends.*

**In The Judges' Eyes:** *Very life-like! Well drawn and well hooked. Great eyes!*

**Not So Fishy Stitches**, 20″ x 16½″, #4- and 5-cut hand-dyed wool on linen.
Designed and hooked by Laurie Wiles, Edmonton, Alberta, 2021.

# Popcorn & Paperhat

Perusing photos I have taken often inspires a possible project. Whatever grips my attention as I page through pictures, floats through my thoughts for days or months and becomes a motivation. Two photos of Amelia at an art show caught my eye. I revisited them many times before deliberately deciding to hook the picture.

The girl and her prized collections from the art show—popcorn and a paper hat— is the story. I hook her on a flattering cotton bouclé fabric that becomes the background support. Hand-dyed wool always works well for hooking, regardless of the chosen backing. A party-favor jewel was perfect for the ring.

The detail is critical. Which details do I keep, which should I edit out? What about the nuances? From eyes to shadows, I hooked what I saw in the chosen photo. Editing a photo or mental visual is always important. Asking the right questions helps. What is necessary? What is extraneous? If I omit this or that, does it change the story? Thinking it through is incredibly important. *Popcorn & Paperhat* is wrapped on a linen canvas, ready to hang.

**Capri Boyle Jones**
Navarre, Florida

*Capri Boyle Jones is owner of Capri Boyle Rug Studio, Navarre, Florida. She is a McGown Certified Instructor and member of ATHA and Guild of Pearl K. McGown Hookrafters. Experienced in all styles, she teaches nationally and locally. You may find her artwork at Quayside Art Gallery in Pensacola, Florida; other galleries and art shows throughout the US, and in private collections.*

**In The Judges' Eyes:** *Wonderful, original design. Well designed and expertly shaded. Very impressive.*

**Popcorn & Paperhat**, 12″ x 30″, hand-dyed wool on cotton bouclé.
Designed and hooked by Capri Boyle Jones, Navarre, Florida, 2021.

# *Regal Emergence*

I was on a safari with my husband in the Masai Mara National Reserve in Kenya. We were hoping to see a leopard and heard about a sighting not far away. Just as we arrived at that location a beautiful two-year old male leopard slowly emerged from an opening in the brush. He was a fair distance away and I was the only one with a telephoto lens. I quickly snapped a few photos before the leopard moved on. Leopards are elusive and difficult to capture on film.

I love the way the arched branch framed the subject in the light, with beautiful foliage in the background. I'm pleased with the front of the leopard and the strong and noble expression on his face.

The wool cut size was from #3 to #7, but I mostly used narrow cuts. This helped in two ways: I was able to capture the detail where it was warranted, and it gave me a larger variety of colors and values to choose from and hook into tiny places.

The leopard's tail was challenging. I had to hook it several times. It had to be hooked in darker values because it was under brush and leaves, but it still had to be distinguishable and not get lost in the greenery. I worked through it by experimenting with darker values and—with persistence— I finally achieved the contrast I needed.

I needed a lot of patience to hook this rug. Every loop had to be specifically placed to achieve the colors and values on the leopard's chest, for example. I also learned if a section does not sit right, do not leave it. Redo it until it is right. Also, I learned how to create a detailed landscape background around a main subject.

**Jane F. Smith**
Orleans, Ontario

*Jane F. Smith has been hooking rugs for four years. She has a background in amateur photography and belongs to the Ottawa Olde Forge Rug Hooking Guild. She loves hooking subjects with a heartbeat and has completed pieces of both her sons and several dogs and cats.*

**In The Judges' Eyes:** *Wonderful use of muted colors. The green eyes are a brilliant touch. Great development of surrounding bush.*

**Regal Emergence**, 28″ x 23″, #3- to 7-cut as-is wool and yarn on linen.
Designed and hooked by Jane F. Smith, Orleans, Ontario, 2021.

# Sand Sea Boardwalk & Me

After a long spell when it seemed I was only hooking skies, I was drawn to hook this precisely because it did not have a sky! I had been hooking non-stop sky since the beginning of 2019. As I was finishing up my Hoboken Sunsets, I went to my idea file and two images caught my eye. One was a watercolor from a Hebridean trip taken decades ago, and the other a picture taken as a rug idea while at the 2018 Cape May Rug Show.

The Hebridean image had…way…too…much…sky! I was so over sky. The other was a cheeky play on my long-percolating thoughts of doing a self-portrait.

I have always hooked with yarn. For me, yarn is the best medium for the painterly approach I take with my rugs, which are about color, pattern, and mood. Quite unintentionally, I am developing a pointillist style of presenting an image, and yarn gives me the points of color that I need.

I particularly like the blowing hair on the left side of my head—successfully rendered and thereby confirming the reality of the entire image. I can almost see the wind passing through my hair.

Why did I not see how intricate the hooking of this boardwalk would be? I went crazy with wood graining. Line after line of single-ply yarn. One very full week of hooking per board. It made me lose my sense of humor and—temporarily—my joy of rug hooking! Yes.

I just kept hooking one line of grain after another. The shadow had to be laid in with each line of grain. Three months of hooking woodgrain! (I will never hook a board again.)

Hooking (creating any Art) for me is always about depth of seeing rather than assuming. One might think they know what woodgrain looks like. But to create it, one has to seriously look. I had to look at the reality of each individual line of wood or swirl of sand. Adding the shadow on top made the intensity of seeing even more necessary. I think I "see" better now that when I started the project, but that generally happens with each project I undertake.

I intended to name this piece *Self Portrait.* This appealed to my general sense of cheekiness. When I showed my in-process rug for the first time at a Zoom rug hooking event, I showed it with little explanation and in pre-planned bits and sections, leaving the photo I was working from to the end. I don't think people had a clue what they were looking at! I needed to tell people what they were seeing. I don't want to, nor should I, show the photo whenever I show the rug. Maybe a more descriptive title would be helpful. Hence—*Sand Sea Boardwalk and Me.*

There was no sea in the original image. I just liked the alliteration of the four-word title. I have been surprised by the sea of sand that emerged from the rug. But it was there in the photo. My eyes saw it, but my brain lagged a few months behind. Fortunately, my hands did my eyes bidding!

**Nancy Thun**
Hoboken, New Jersey

*Nancy Thun found her way into rug hooking in 2009 when she saw someone hooking with yarn. Now she could spend her entire day hooking and binge-watching TV! A set designer, she works on Broadway and internationally, with London-based designers.*

**In The Judges' Eyes:** *Incredible use of design elements. The shadow colors and shading are exceptional. Superb use of medium in bold expression.*

1st Place

**Sand Sea Boardwalk and Me**, 34″ x 49″, hand-dyed wool yarn on rug warp.
Designed and hooked by Nancy Thun, Hoboken, New Jersey, 2021.

# Spiraling

Rug hooking became my way to process emotions during 2020 and 2021. I found joy as bold colors emerged from the dye pot. Then, rhythmically hooking the strips of wool into a tactile artwork was calming and cathartic. This rug depicts emotions experienced with the pandemic, political, and societal concerns during 2020 and 2021.

The image originated as a 2″ x 2″ doodle that I found in one of my old sketchbooks. In the image, waves of overwhelming emotion accumulate as a cloud over the head of the individual, while thoughts spiral in confusion atop a posture of despair. Strong, angular contrast in the midsection denotes the anxiety experienced—similar to knots in the stomach. The echoing of the hooking radiating out from the dark cloud emphasizes the movement of emotion *from* the person as well as *back toward* the person. The spare, bold palette of red, black, gray, and off-white wool call out for the viewer's attention. The off-white background surrounds the image with a color of hope. Yet, the thin black border suggests a surrounding box from which the individual still needs to remove herself.

Fortunately, since that original doodle, I have experienced and know that hope is the more powerful emotion.

I wanted to capture the bold color of the original doodle (which was done with a basic pack of Crayola markers). I also dyed the red and gray so the colors would be subtly mottled with gradations to add some depth to the stark color scheme.

The negative space within the gray cloud around the head created some unexpected flow and imagery that enhances the piece. On the right side I discovered a stylized sprout with two emerging leaves–perhaps a subliminal symbol of growth and hope. This was the first time that I tackled a rug this large. To create the impact of emotion that the image suggested, I knew it required an almost life-size enlargement. Hooking and watching the boldly colored central image take shape was exciting.

Persevering through hooking the off-white background was challenging, but I was motivated to reach my goal of completion because I believed in the relevance of this piece and the impact it could have on others.

What did I learn? In planning for a large rug, I had to be sure to dye enough wool for each color, and dye the pieces of wool for each color consistently. I learned to keep going even when I wasn't sure. Was my technique okay? Were my loops consistent enough? Would the spiral lay flat? (Yes, after it was steamed.) And, thanks to those experienced rug hookers who have made YouTube videos, held Zoom classes, or have a blog or social media presence, I was able to research some of the information during pandemic restrictions.

I learned that rug hooking can be a very forgiving medium in which to make mistakes. There were many areas that weren't quite what I wanted and I had to redo. This part of the process helped me grow personally, as well as in my rug hooking experience.

Through the approachable textile art of rug hooking, I found my voice. After the months of enduring isolations and quarantines and getting by with Zoom classes and social-media learning, it was connecting in person with Susan Feller and the generous-spirited rug hookers in her retreat at Rug Hooking Week at Sauder Village that finally gave this piece (and me) the confidence of its voice.

As a first-time Rug Hooking Week attendee, I was so grateful for the kindness and helpfulness of the rug-hooking community. Especially valuable was the rich interaction within the retreat; the experience of peer support and sharing during critiques was so meaningful, and an important part of my growth as a rug hooker. In fact, this experience has led me to continue developing this series of images through rug hooking as my chosen medium.

**Terri Todd**
Forest, Virginia

*Terri Todd is retired from teaching elementary-age children. She continues to be inspired by the genuine creativity of children and is grateful for the inspiration found in the beauty of the nearby Blue Ridge Mountains.*

**In The Judges' Eyes:** *Great modern design, terrific. Bold, contemporary colors and design well executed. Technically perfect, as needed for the subject's graphic quality.*

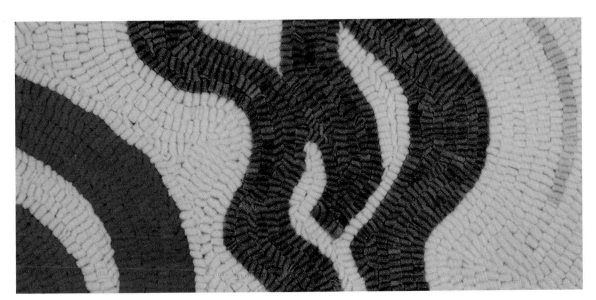

**Spiraling**, 48″ x 48″, #8-cut hand-dyed and as-is wool on linen.
Designed and hooked by Terri Todd, Forest, Virginia, 2021.

# Summer Journey

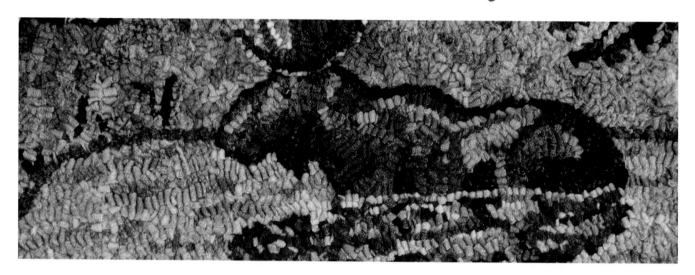

During the summer of 2020, we traveled across the United States and saw wonderful places along the way. I decided to design a rug that included our RV home and the experiences of the trip.

At first I thought to have separate vignettes to depict individual locations from five different states scattered around in one rug. But then I wondered what would happen if I just put them all together—as if the sightings were all in one place, one landscape? I had it pictured in my mind and thought it would work, but when I excitedly discussed it with my in-home art critic, he wasn't so sure. I decided that it was my artistic exploration and I would go for it anyway.

I gathered photos that I had taken during the summer and played with moving them around until they became a cohesive piece. This design includes the Delicate Arch and petroglyphs from Utah; an ancient bristlecone pine tree from California; Rocky Mountains and moose from Colorado; Chimney Rock from Nebraska; and cacti, jackrabbit and rattlesnake from Arizona (that rattlesnake went right through our campsite while I was sitting outside!). I included the Comet NEOWISE, which was so bright that we could see it clearly in the dark Utah sky. The rainbow we saw in Canyonlands when my brother was dying— that rainbow almost didn't make it into the rug because I took it to

mean he would get better. But it was an incredible sight and meaningful moment filled with hope and promise that had to be included. Even the colorful clouds that separate the daytime from the night sky were based on a gorgeous sunset that we saw in Rocky Mountain National Park. Finally, I added silhouettes of Matt and me hiking, since that is one of our favorite ways to explore.

The moose with his reflection was difficult. I referred to the photo that we took through our spotting scope to see the highlights and shadows and made sure I hooked them first. To figure out the reflection, I turned the photo upside down and flipped it on the computer. Having a print to work with helped me to figure it out.

This rug taught me that if I have an out-of-the-box idea that others think is crazy, I should go for it anyway. I really had no clue how this would turn out, or if it would make any sense. But I've found that other people love looking at it and finding things that they have seen—or talking about what it means. It excites people and encourages them to be crazy with their rugs and explorations.

Often, I feel like I am a conduit of creativity: like it is flowing through me, not from me. I found it's best when I stop overthinking, when I just get out of the way and run with the ideas that come to me. This rug is an example of just that.

**Janine Broscious**
Jefferson, Maryland

*Janine Broscious is a retired homeschooling mom who now roams the country in her RV. She enjoys rug hooking, jewelry making, writing, and photography. When she began rug hooking in 2014, she found her creative home.*

**In The Judges' Eyes:** *Wonderful memories well put together. Many elements well placed. Pleasing color plan makes this a lovely memory rug.*

**Summer Journey,** 44" x 27", #3- to 8-cut as-is and hand-dyed wool on linen.
Designed and hooked by Janine Broscious, Jefferson, Maryland, 2020.

# Sunday Best

I had created a watercolor painting from an old black-and-white photo of my maternal relatives and thought it would be a challenge to transform that painting into a painting done in wool.

The variety of textures and colors were adapted to colors similar to the watercolor paint palette.

My great-grandmother is on the right, with her son next to her. These two people I grew up with and was quite familiar with. I knew their features and couldn't fudge on the details. Having them come alive on the linen was satisfying. I love how their garments and features stayed true to who they were.

The details of the facial features were quite difficult. I studied my painting and tried to transpose the brush strokes, shadows, and detail by using wool. With the wool, you cannot be as detailed as with paint and canvas—you need to imply color placement and depth. Making a one-dimensional linen foundation reflect depth, contour, and transition is tedious, accomplished by manipulation of the wool. Using different-size cuts and placing those cuts just right can transform a flat surface.

I applied a "show finish" for the edge of the rug, using a brown tweed herringbone wool fabric that would reflect a man's suit fabric.

What did I learn in hooking this rug? I learned patience! The study of the human face and body—along with draping—was a big learning curve for me. You absolutely need to "hook what you see, not what you think you see."

Life hasn't been the same since.

I encourage everyone to try your hand at documenting an important moment in time in the form of a rug. These memory rugs will become heirlooms for future generations.

**Valerie Begeman**
Rapid City, South Dakota

*Introduced to the art of traditional rug hooking in 2006 by her mother, Valerie Begeman has explored all aspects of rug hooking since then. Attaining her McGown Accreditation in 2018, she belongs to ATHA, the Guild of Pearl K. McGown Hookrafters, and the Mount Rushmore Rug Hookers' Social Club in Rapid City, South Dakota.*

**In The Judges' Eyes:** *Beautiful translation of a photograph. Sweet memories in wool. From watercolor to fiber art—excellent!*

JOHNNY SUNDBY

**Sunday Best**, 25" x 17", #4-, 6-, and 8-cut hand-dyed and as-is wool on linen.
Designed and hooked by Valerie Begeman, Rapid City, South Dakota, 2021.

# The Bridge at Cushendun

I took the photo in 2005 on a trip around County Antrim, Northern Ireland. The village of Cushendun on the River Dun, the bridge, and the Giant's Causeway stood out in my memories of the land my Kilpatrick ancestors left when they emigrated in 1825. This is the first of a Kilpatrick trilogy.

I had a wide selection of tans and peach-colored wools picked out for the bridge, but a single piece of a spot dye from Michele Micarelli made hooking the bridge a breeze. Each loop pulled was like a separate stone in the bridge. I found a wonderful murky spot dye of grays and dark teals and recognized it as the "water under the bridge." I only used a small bit of it, but it was perfect!

Plaids and textures played important roles in the water and the top edge of the bridge. A tiny strip of a synthetic fabric added just a touch of sparkle to the dark water under the bridge.

Capturing the wind-riffled texture of the water moving into more smooth-flowing water in the foreground was fun. I especially like the reflections of the stone bridge in the rippling water. I had to focus on hooking what I saw in the photo—myriad reflections broken by the wind. I had to think of it not as "water," but as "bridge" and "cloud" reflected and sparkling on the surface.

Getting the lacy feel of the large trees on the right stumped me for a while. A technique used in the water worked: Pull two different #3 strips at once. In the water, this helped with the fine rippled texture; in the trees, one dark-green and one sky-blue were hooked together and then manipulated to create the tree/sky lace.

I put my 8″ x 10″ photo in a ziplock bag on which I drew a 1″ grid. On my linen, I added a 3″ grid over the pattern lines, and that helped me focus on one square at a time and hook the details.

My grandmother had made a few hooked rugs that were in the house where I grew up. They were simple geometrics in browns and grays; she got wool remnants from an uncle who worked for Hart Schaffner Marx, a men's suit company. I've always appreciated the re-use and re-purposing of materials, and much of my wool stash comes out of thrift stores. I recently spotted some Hart Schaffner Marx trousers!

In 2012 or so, I took a trip to Nova Scotia and happened upon a local show of hooked art. I visited Encompassing Designs in Mahone Bay and bought a book, a hook, and a piece of linen. I made a few chair pads using leftover fabrics from my sewing stash—including the 3″ hem cut off my skirt in 1969 when the dress code changed to allow skirts above, rather than below, the knee. I might have quit then, but I ran into a friend who said, "Oh, I'm a hooker too, and we meet twice a month. . ." The social aspect made all the difference, and rug hooking has become my main creative endeavor.

**Barbara Ackemann**
Brattleboro, Vermont

*Barbara Ackemann grew up with her grandmother's hooked rugs. In her retirement she took up rug hooking after a trip to Nova Scotia. She hooks with the Brattleboro Area Rug Social group and is on the board of the Green Mountain Rug Hooking Guild.*

**In The Judges' Eyes:** *Lovely design elements well placed. The bridge has great depth, with expert shading and good contrast. Wow!*

**The Bridge at Cushendun**, 22″ x 30″, #3- to 6-cut hand-dyed and as-is wool and wool yarn on linen.
Designed and hooked by Barb Ackemann, Brattleboro, Vermont, 2021.

# The British Are Coming

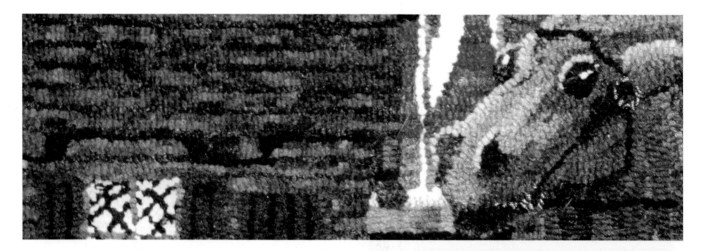

A spontaneous trip to Boston in 2018—where we got lost trying to find Paul Revere's house and then afterward couldn't stop finding the house—and of course the poem "Paul Revere's Ride," by Henry Wadsworth Longfellow, were the inspiration.

A #3 cut is my favorite size to work with. Swatches and texture packs were used for the shaded pieces, including the horse and the jacket, the lit windows on the house, and the church. Spot dyes made the perfect texture for the grass and dirt and house, while plaids became a good replication for the bricks on the church and the shingles on the house. And a tiny bit of shiny fabric was used on the metals bit of the tack on the horse and for the unlit window of the house.

The drawing of the horse on the initial pattern was a challenge, especially since I don't tend to use transfer material. I prefer to draw right on the backing, so I needed to make sure that looked proper from the get-go.

With this rug, I learned, once again, to trust my instincts. If something scares you, try it anyway. And don't be afraid to try colors, sometimes a lot of colors—even colors that you may not think belong there.

I sell patterns under the name Lost Leaf Designs. I would like to turn this into a series of popular misquoted sayings.

### Melissa McKay
Stettler, Alberta

*Melissa McKay lives in a small town in central Alberta and has been lucky to have great rug hooking resources nearby, such as Hot Off the Hook Rug Group in Rocky Mountain House, Alberta.*

**In The Judges' Eyes:** *Architectural elements and flags waving give a primitive yet realistic feel. Delightful colors with good contrast give life and movement to this picture. Flag border adds just the right touch of patriotism.*

**The British Are Coming**, 24″ x 41″, #3- and 5-cut hand-dyed and as-is wool and alternative materials on linen. Designed and hooked by Melissa McKay, Stettler, Alberta, 2021.

# The El Mocambo

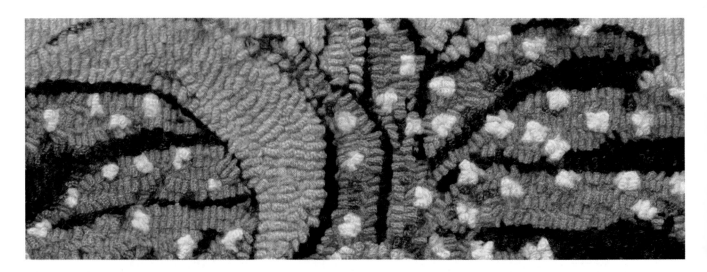

The El Mocambo is a live music venue in Toronto that I used to frequent in my youth. The El Mocambo closed for renovation and was due to reopen in the spring of 2020, but that was postponed by the pandemic. It has been a difficult time for musicians. Musicians like an audience. I think visual artists and musicians should support each other.

This is an intimate venue, but big-name musicians have played here, including The Rolling Stones, Elvis Costello, Stevie Ray Vaughn, and The Ramones. It is legendary. It opened in 1948. My mother went there. She had an El Mocambo swizzle stick in her collection.

Even before the pandemic, Toronto had seen an alarming number of venues close their doors. It is a loss to the city if creative people must leave. But this story has a happy ending. The El Mocambo has survived and recently re-opened.

I use wool from garments that I find at thrift shops. Sometimes that means you have a special piece of wool that no one else has. I hooked this rug from my stash, except for the Briggs & Little charcoal-gray wool that I ordered for curbside pick-up from Romni Wools.

I like the brickwork. I found pieces of wool in my stash that were a herringbone tweed overdyed with pink mahogany on one end and a rusty orange at the other end, with a blending of the two dyes in the middle. The texture of the tweed adds depth to the color.

It was challenging to keep the rug square. It wasn't until I measured and photographed the rug that I realized it's a little out of whack. This is because the sky is hooked in straight horizontal rows, and the brickwork has a diagonal thrust to it. I had a finite amount of brick-colored wool, so I didn't want to re-hook that. I felt that I needed the brickwork to follow the lines of perspective and that it was necessary to keep the diagonal hooking. I re-hooked the sky but, in the end, I accepted that it was never going to be as square as I would like it to be. In the future I will avoid designing rugs that need this diagonal hooking.

Most of my work is concerned with telling a story, but I also hook rugs that are experiments in color and composition. I began hooking rugs about the Maritimes—my grandmother's and my mother's stories. Lately I have begun to tell my own story. Many of my newer rugs are about the city of Toronto, where I live with my husband and my cat. I think of my work as a visual diary. This is my COVID-19 project.

## Trish Johnson
Toronto, Ontario

*Trish Johnson has been hooking rugs for 31 years. She goes weekly to the Upper Toronto branch of the Ontario Hooking Craft Guild. Her rugs are in the Celebration Hall of Fame.*

**In The Judges' Eyes:** *Unique and artistically interesting concept in this design. Rich colors add warmth and a general feeling of fun. The perspective is well done. Great rendition. The lights on the palm leaves seem to glow!*

GRAEME FLANNIGAN

**The El Mocambo**, 17″ x 26½″, #4- and 6-cut hand-dyed and as-is wool on linen.
Designed and hooked by Trish Johnson, Toronto, Ontario, 2021.

# These City Walls

I had signed up for a pictorial class with Linda Powell. Before the class, I was on a trip in Vilnius, Lithuania, which is a UNESCO Heritage Site. Walking outside the city walls, I took several pictures. One of these was a doorway in the wall. The photo of the door itself was too large, so I cropped a very small area which I then made into my design.

For this piece I hit the dye pots. I dyed dozens of different of shades of rust and close to 50 shades of gray. In both of these colors, I went for very light to very dark. This high contrast adds a lot more visual interest. The colors that I used were nearly identical to the photo.

The section I love the most is the iron bar, for four reasons. First, the iron bar is the color in a mostly neutral palette. Second, the iron bar has the finest detail, particularly in the bolts and in the hinge. Third, the shadows under the bolts provide depth. Fourth, the high contrast in values provide visual interest and realism.

The iron bar was also the most challenging section because

of the difficulty hooking the element of rust. I worked through this challenge by having a wide range of values in the rust-dyed wool. My visual aid was an important reference that I referred to constantly.

I did not put a border on this piece. I turned back the linen, much like Roslyn Logsdon does to finish her rugs. I then added black cotton tape, which was sewn right up to the loops, then, on the other side, tacked down through to the backing..

Every piece is a learning piece. With this rug I learned how important it is to have high contrast. It was also important to have a large variety of values for depth. Also, the visual is so important—really, really study all the details!

A quilting friend showed me how to pull up a loop. She gave me a piece of burlap and a hook and told me to draw my own pattern. Since then, I have taken many classes and obtained teaching accreditations. I also quilt, knit, bead, and do creative stitching and needlework.

**Val Flannigan**
Kelowna, British Columbia

*Val Flannigan is totally hooked on rug hooking. She considers herself a lifelong learner, and she is planning to design many more rug from photos of her travels.*

**In The Judges' Eyes:** *Wonderful concept for a rug. The colors and shading give real depth. Wonderful! A perfect example of realism through details in hooking. This is an amazing piece.*

**These City Walls**, 17″ x 23″, #4-cut hand dyed wool on linen.
Designed and hooked by Val Flannigan, Kelowna, British Columbia, 2021.

# Urban Icons

My ideas come from life observations, and I use them to create story-art pieces. The original concept morphs over time as I add layers of meaning, much like creating a collage of ideas. One idea builds on the next—adding complexity to the overall composition, making the story more readable.

I lived in the Denver area of Colorado for many years where my daughter owned two day-labor agencies that provided temporary work situations for homeless men and women who wanted to work. There I was exposed to the many American veterans and people with mental illness and alcohol/drug addictions who make up the homeless community. I wanted to tell their stories in a graphic way through fiber art: their lives on the streets, extreme poverty, mental illness, drug addiction, and in a very real way having their survival depend on a society that shuns and marginalizes them.

This rug is full of symbols, and all of the figures in this rug are female.

- The string of rocks around one woman's neck symbolizes the weight and baggage of mental illness.

- The halo around the central figure's head is created with tiny transistors that look like pills, symbolizing addiction.

- The other figures in this rug have Milagros or "miracles" sewn into the backing – protective symbols that serve to tell the story of the hazards of living on the streets.

- There is an appliqué that makes reference to the Beatitudes.

- The craft-beer and soda caps that surround this rug symbolize a society that surrounds but steers clear of the homeless.

- My grandson, Russell, created the design for the graffiti.

Hand-dyed wools are used to create the appliqué and graffiti background. The figures are all hooked and sculpted in wool. I used an onion bag to create the bag that hangs from the shopping cart, representing bags of recycled aluminum cans. Other pieces of fabric are attached to the background in the form of paint spatters, and there is a piece of cotton fabric hanging from the cart.

I love all the different aspects of the piece. It was very engaging and interesting to work on, but I acknowledge that I am partial to the woman with the stones around her neck. Her face really reflects her addiction and the abuses she endures while being homeless. Her eyes are squinting as she looks at the audience with distrust and animosity.

Finding a way to attach the bottle caps was a challenge. I knew I did not want to use glue. At first, I intended to pierce each cap and use wire as the attachment but decided that might cut through the linen backing over time. In the end I used a heavy waxed-linen thread to attach the pierced caps one by one.

*Urban Icons* is a large and heavy rug. I whipstitched rug-tape strips vertically, from top to bottom every six inches across the back of the rug, to help distribute the weight. The rug-tape strips terminate at the top, forming loops from which to hang the rug on a rod.

## Cheryl Bollenbach
### Eads, Tennessee

*Cheryl Bollenbach has a degree in art and majored in sculpture. She started rug hooking in 2005 and quickly began to sculpt the hooked wool to give it dimension. She is a McGown Certified Instructor, and the editor for ATHA magazine. She teaches nationally and sells hand-dyed wool from her home studio.*

**In The Judges' Eyes:** *Love that this rugger may have known some of these ladies and honored them with portraits. Colors are lovely, idea unique, and love the border. Powerful symbols, mixed media, and expert hooking make this a dramatic statement.*

**Urban Icons**, 60″ x 52″, hand-dyed wool, needle-felted roving, appliqué, and mixed-media embellishments on linen. Designed and hooked by Cheryl Bollenbach, Eads, Tennessee, 2020.

# Women's Voices, Women's Right to Vote

2019 marked the 100th anniversary of the ratification of the 19th Amendment, giving American women the right to vote. I wanted to celebrate that achievement and to honor Susan B. Anthony, a leader of the movement.

I dyed wool in the two colors that the Suffragettes used in their movement: purple and gold. I used #3 cuts to give me flexibility to create the small details. And the colors work well with each other because they're complements.

I love how Susan B. Anthony's face turned out. She was strong, dedicated, and devoted to her cause, and she looks serious and tough. This rug represents her accomplishment and her role in making it happen.

There is a line of women voters, each one representing twenty years of their right to vote. I researched women's fashions so I could dress them accordingly. Getting those details in small figures was tricky, but I think it works.

I designed it with an arched top to create a marquee-style frame; when the hooking was complete, I whipped the edges with yarn I dyed to match the purple in the rug.

I learned as an artist that I can create a split-monochromatic rug with two colors represented in their own range of values. And as a woman, I learned that women have to fight for their rights and that perseverance pays off.

My friends in Kindred Spirits got me started in rug hooking twenty years ago. I was reluctant to try it, but once I did, I fell for it completely and have never looked back.

I enjoy working with oils, watercolors, and colored pencils. During the COVID shutdown, I collaborated with my youngest son to illustrate a card game he created. I did the artwork based on his vision of the characters and what he wanted the game to look like. It was fun, challenging, and really rewarding.

Rug hooking is my artistic voice, and being recognized for my work is very gratifying and rewarding.

### Donna K. Hrkman
Dayton, Ohio

*Donna K. Hrkman has been an artist since childhood, and rug hooking is her joy. She's won awards and recognition for her work and has written three books. Donna teaches across the country and loves sharing what she knows.*

**In The Judges' Eyes:** *Great use of yellow and purple. A rug hooking masterpiece. Amazing detail, love the side columns.*

Women's Voices, Women's Right to Vote, 26″ x 36″, #3-cut hand-dyed wool on linen.
Designed and hooked by Donna K. Hrkman, Dayton, Ohio, 2020.

DAN HRKMAN

# Burnham Floral

I was inspired by one of the first rug hookers I ever met, Connie Tisdahl, from Fergus Falls, Minnesota, who hooked this design. She had seen the pattern offered free in RHM; Annie Spring's beautiful rendition was featured in that issue. I remember Connie saying, "I can do that." Well, I wasn't sure I could ever do it, but when Max Bowers offered to sell me her pattern drawn on monk's cloth, I considered it fate.

I started working on it at Prairie Rose Rug School held at Assumption Abbey, a monastery in Richardton, North Dakota. I love hooking there, with the peaceful atmosphere and view of the prairie. Ingrid Hieronimus was my teacher. She gave me the best lesson I've ever had on hooking roses using the fingering technique. Then she advised me: whatever colors I chose, just keep moving them around, and it will be beautiful.

For materials I gathered treasures from my stash, including some Prisms swatches and dip dyes that were dyed by Ingrid. Ingrid's dyed wool is irresistible. Her dye books and samples are frequently my starting point if I need to do my own dyeing.

I found this entire design challenging. I kept Ingrid's advice in mind and moved the colors around. The most challenging aspect was the sheer number of leaves. My pep talk to myself was that I was going to be a lot better at hooking leaves by the time I finished this design.

My hooking career started in 1998 after seeing a hooked piece in a quilt shop. In 2012, the Red Door Art Gallery in Wahpeton featured an exhibit of my hooked rugs. I'm happy that these old-favorite designs have been preserved for posterity.

**Terryl Ostmo**
Wahpeton, North Dakota

*Terryl Ostmo has been hooking rugs since 1998 and became a McGown Certified Instructor in 2012. She plans to keep hooking for as long as she is able. She enjoys hooking pretty much anything: florals, geometries, people, and animals.*

**In The Judges' Eyes:** *Vivid color use excellent. Bright colors are stunning again. Dark background and shading is excellent. Bright rainbow colors handled well.*

**Burnham Floral**, 32″ x 58″, #3-cut hand-dyed wool on monk's cloth.
Designed by Jane McGown Flynn and hooked by Terryl Ostmo, Wahpeton, North Dakota, 2021.

# Florabella

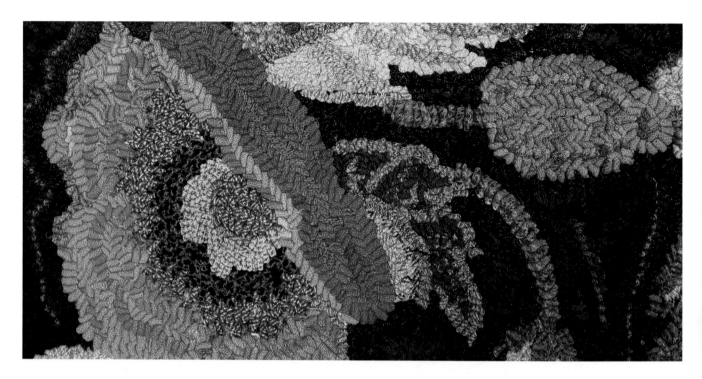

I loved this pattern with brightly-colored flowers—poppies, morning glories, and buttercups, to name a few. I love gardening and try to incorporate many bright, bold colors into my landscaping. This rug reminds me of my garden, even on cold winter days here in northwestern Illinois.

I wanted to learn how to shade using wide cuts. I was encouraged by teachers to use cut strips of wool in my stash from previous projects within the dark background and darker areas around the edge of the rug. I learned that using wool from other projects does two things: It saves the rug hooker money, and it uses up some of that stash that we all have so much of. What a great idea! I was able to utilize a variety of recycled pieces of wool clothing in this rug, saving even more money.

I learned how to shade using wide-cut strips of wool. I also learned a lot of valuable tips, like how to save money by using recycled wool clothing and wool from other projects. I learned how to give the background movement by using leftover wool in shades other than just black. In addition to the black wool in the background, there are purples, blues, and greens.

It all started with my mother-in-law gifting me my first rug hooking kit back in 1991. My kids were all very young back then and kept me busy, so I stashed it away. I finally brought it out in 2013, when learning how to hook was a godsend. My health took a turn for the worse, and I was no longer able to create fine needlework. Rug hooking is something I can do as long as I have my bent-shaft rug hook. That hook was given to me by a fellow rug hooker who just happened to be an occupational therapist. Rug hooking has given me a creative outlet. I am grateful to my mother-in-law, Marion Lardner, who is also a rug hooker, for encouraging me to take up the art of rug hooking.

**Linnea Christine Lardner**
Milan, Illinois

*Linnea Christine Lardner has been hooking rugs since 2013 and is basically a self-taught beginner who has taken classes over the years. Through all the classes and events, she's met and befriended rug hookers from all over the country.*

**In The Judges' Eyes:** *Stunning colors. Well hooked. Colors harmonize beautifully.*

**Florabella**, 40″ x 56″, #8-, 8.5-, 9-cut and hand-torn wool strips, recycled wool clothing, as-is and hand-dyed wool, and antique paisley. Designed by Joanne Gerwig and hooked by Linnea Christine Lardner, Milan, Illinois, 2021.

# Floral Sampler

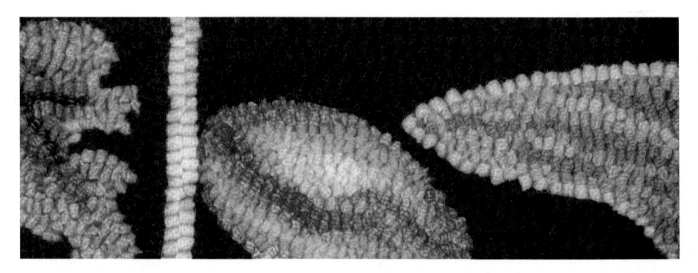

This rug was designed by Jane McGown Flynn, and she presented the dahlia, tulip, daffodil, and rose impressively. I tried to use colors and hooking technique in these glamorous flowers that kept each individual image distinct. In the dahlia, I used two types of red swatches, using the double-swatch technique. That allowed me to express the deep glamour of this flower. For the tulip, I used transitional-dyed wool, changing its color from red to yellow. That allowed me to make natural color transitions in the petals. For the daffodil, I used swatch-dyed wool to show the flower as it would naturally bloom. I thought of the rose as a variety called Blue Rose, which is light purple and very fragrant. I imagined those roses as I was hooking.

I really enjoyed hooking these flowers. Every time I hook natural flowers, I find something new. There are many ways to hook flowers, and I learned a lot from this pattern. I learned that, before hooking, it is important to have an image of the complete rug. I learned to decide what dyeing method to use, and I learned I must choose how to hook this rug—realistic, artistic, or primitive.

I took the time to hook the dahlia with double-swatched wool. I thought it wise to put many colors in each petal. Using a double swatch was my new challenge.

I used a double swatch of two reds for the dahlia. Using this method, I thought I could show off the dahlia with depth in the petals and make the flower gorgeous.

For the tulip on the right, I used transitional-dyed wool. To show them as they are in nature, I made the colors in the petals change from red to yellow.

When I was a child, my mother made a rug using a latch-hook kit. It was interesting for me to see how yarn could turn into a picture. Many years later, I found rug hooking through the internet. Also appealing to me is that this craft was born from a wisdom of life, using recycled fabrics, yarns, and burlap. As I learned more and my interest grew, I began to search for a teacher. I met Chizuko Hayami, became a student of hers that very same day, and remain her student to this day.

**Yoshiho Nara**
Tokyo, Japan

*Yoshiho Nara has been hooking for seven years. She has hooked 60 rugs to date. She is a rug hooking teacher at Chizuko Rug Hooking Studio in Tokyo, is a member of the Guild of Pearl K. McGown Hookrafters, and is a McGown Certified Instructor.*

**In The Judges' Eyes:** *Superior shading! Excellent use of color. Stunning rug.*

**Floral Sampler**, 16″ x 16″, #3-cut hand-dyed wool on linen.
Designed by Jane McGown Flynn and hooked by Yoshiho Nara, Tokyo, Japan, 2020.

# Folk Fraktur
# Robin Redbreast Bird Nest

This was a wedding gift for my son and daughter-in-law. When I first saw this lovely fraktur-style pattern online, I thought it would be something they would like–and they did. The designer agreed to enlarge the pattern to make it the desired finished size. To make the pattern my own, I made a few design changes to the original. I added extra linen on all four edges to add a border, made a few flower adjustments, and added two bees, as the couple are beekeepers.

There are probably 80-plus different wools in this piece. Most of the wool I use is textured, as it blends well with other wools, and I find using many wools adds interest and dimension.

The technique used on the nest I learned at my very first rug hooking retreat; it is basically proddy. I wanted to add some dimension and interest to the nest, so I randomly hooked assorted short wool strips, leaving about one inch at the start and end. The raised strips were thinned out by pulling off the cross threads with the edge of embroidery scissors and cutting off a few threads here and there until I was happy with the look.

Initially I wasn't sure what colors to use in the arched set of triangles connected to the sun. After considering several possibilities, I selected the colors already used in the pattern, and placed them in a color progression to resemble a rainbow. I repeated this pattern in the border, using the sun design in all four corners. For the background, I echo-hooked, alternating neutral and muted colors from the pattern. I believe this adds another design element to the rug.

**Jill Hicks**
Valparaiso, Indiana

*Jill Hicks loves being creative and has worked with many fiber arts; however, rug hooking is what she enjoys the most. Now that her children are all grown, she has more time to pursue her passion.*

**In The Judges' Eyes:** *Pretty color use, appropriate for a fraktur. Colors are pleasing. Great birds and nest.*

**Folk Fraktur Robin Redbreast Bird Nest**, 43″x 40″, #6-cut as-is, hand-dyed, and recycled wool on linen.
Designed by Michelle Palmer and hooked by Jill Hicks, Valparaiso, Indiana, 2021.

# Fruit Medley

I first saw this pattern when my guild, Buffalo Trace Rug Hookers, completed it as a group project to raffle off in support of the 2009 Biennial held in Louisville, Kentucky. I didn't win that raffle, so I had to hook one myself! I learned so much throughout this process, and it challenged my wool-dyeing skills.

The back-story of the dye formula I used to get the watermelon flesh color is this: I found the formula in a 1958 edition of *Rugger's Roundtable* newsletter, by Mildred Sprout. The recipe used Cushing dyes. The remarkable part is that all the dye names called-for in the recipe are still produced by Cushing today, and I got exactly the color I was hoping for on the first try. To encounter this product consistency some 65-plus years later was reassuring.

The pieces of fruit that required smooth transitions of color were very challenging, especially the pears, apples, and peaches. Getting

those "in-between" colors can be hard to find in a wool stash! This prompted me to research older rug hooking publications for help. I found a wool-dyeing technique illustrated by Joan Moshimer in a 1975 issue of *The Rug Hooker News and Views* that proved to be the key for me. While she refers to it as a casserole spot dye, to me it seemed closer to what we would describe today as "painting" the wool, with intentional placement of the different colors that were needed onto one piece of wool. Essentially, lay the wool flat, and then blend those colors into each other to create those in-between colors that aid in a smooth transition from one featured color to another.

I replaced a squirrel motif that was in one corner of the original pattern with an additional grouping of strawberries. That helped me balance the reds across the design.

**Tammy Godwin**
Louisville, Kentucky

*Tammy Godwin learned to hook in 2000. She is a member of Buffalo Trace Rug Hookers Guild in Louisville as well as a member of ATHA. She enjoys using all widths of wool strips, and especially enjoys trying to achieve subtle color detail using narrower cuts.*

**In The Judges' Eyes:** *Wonderful use of colors, so pleasing to look at. Lovely interpretation, well shaded. Every fruit well executed.*

**Fruit Medley**, 56″ x 15″, #3- and 4-cut wool on linen.
Designed by Salma Dhanji and hooked by Tammy Godwin, Louisville, Kentucky, 2021.

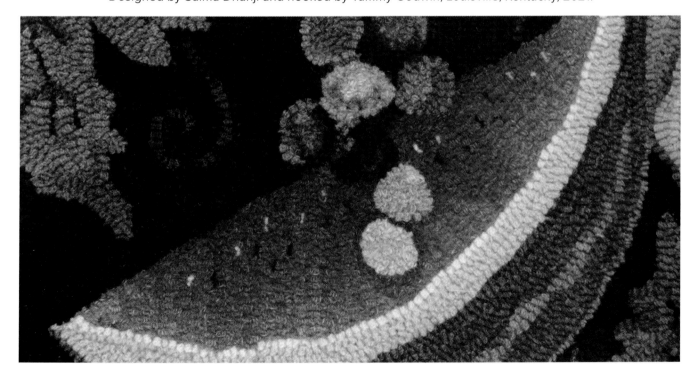

# Hansel and Gretel Cottage

This pattern is based on the illustration by Kay Nielsen for a Grimm fairy tale. I like that this illustration has a feeling of a stage set with depth. So I wanted to express an image of a cottage made of sweets that suddenly appears in a deep forest, spot lit on stage. I hooked the cottage made of sweets brightly and cheerfully and warmly, and the trees around it as a cold and dark forest, mysterious and terrifying.

This pattern was more difficult than I first thought it would be. Hooking it taught me many things, such as devising a new dyeing method for the trees, searching for the destination of intertwined branches, hooking tiny motifs on the door, expressing fluttering smoke from the chimney and more. I often had to stop and think and plan, and trial-and-error got me to the end.

The main decision was deciding the color for the trees in the forest, which makes up so much of the design. In order to express this mysterious forest, I devised a dyeing method for the wool. I dyed a 6-value spot-dye on elongated wool strips, then I added dip dyeing. This method produced a gradient wool with some spots. I used three types of wool dyed by this method to hook other trees in the forest that were not spot lit.

**Kyoko Okamura**
Nerima-ku, Tokyo, Japan

*Kyoko Okamura has enjoyed rug hooking since 2001. She teaches at the Chizuko Rug Hooking Studio and is a McGown Certified Instructor.*

**In The Judges' Eyes:** *Excellent use of color and shading evoke depth. Technique and finishing are exceptional. Close viewing show interesting detail and pops of color.*

JUN KONTA

**Hansel and Gretel Cottage**, 25″ x 34″, #2- to 4-cut hand-dyed and textured wool on linen. Designed by Kay Nielsen and hooked by Kyoko Okamura, Nerima-ku, Tokyo, Japan, 2021.

# Her Constant Companion

The colors and intricate design were a challenge. I tried to stay true to the design and the colors used by the artist.

My favorite part to hook was the tiny face. But it is difficult to choose a favorite when the whole design is so intriguing and complicated. It is all good.

What did I learn as I hooked this rug? Infinite patience.

I am a lover of all things handmade. I am an avid quilter and have always loved handmade rugs. In fact, I think handmade quilts and rugs are like peanut butter and jelly. My life is joyful and will continue to be so as long as I can hook rugs.

**Dell Higley**
Elk Grove, California

*Dell Higley is 85 years old and has been rug hooking 18 years. She has been quilting and teaching for over 40 years. These two art forms have given her great joy.*

**In The Judges' Eyes:** *Brilliant and contrasting colors add drama. Nice interpretation of a complex design. Bright palette handled well.*

**Her Constant Companion,** 35"x 28", #3-, 4-, and 6-cut wool on linen.
Designed by David Galchutt and hooked by Dell Higley, Elk Grove, California, 2021.

# Little Buckingham

My mother and I were enjoying a day off work, attending a hook-in, about thirty years ago when I first came upon this pattern. After window shopping at all the attending vendor booths, the last vendor I came across had something that caught my eye. I had spotted an interesting box which contained a wonderful floral pattern with directions for color placement and all the wool needed for the motifs; all I had to do was rip out and re-hook a couple of lily petals and dye a background. How could I pass up this "kit" for the low, low price of twenty-two dollars?

Fifteen years later I finally pulled the *Little Buckingham* box out of storage and took it to rug camp, where it would have my undivided attention. By the end of the week, I had a good start on all the flower motifs and leaves—and had not only purchased my background wool but had a dye plan as well. I also discovered that there was not enough wool for one style of leaf. This led me to try to replicate the formula given in the color-plan information. My first attempt to match those leaves left me less than satisfied, so I tried again with better success. I now felt I could easily use both dip-dyed batches.

So why did I end up packing away *Little Buckingham* in its box for ten more years? Life sometimes gets in the way and causes us to refocus priorities. For me, it meant having to live through the untimely passing of family members and adjusting to retirement before I again pulled out the box to take to another rug camp.

I now discovered that I didn't like the color of the strap leaves. I decided to incorporate the wools of the other leaves instead of bringing in another color. I also found that I didn't have enough wool to hook all the gloxinia-type tubular flowers. So I returned home to again attempt replicating the dyed wool from the formula given in the included color plan. I was more successful this time and was able to complete the gloxinias with the original swatch and the newly-dyed gloxinia swatch.

Unfortunately, other rugs became greater priorities and again *Little Buckingham* was packed away for another five years. This time, it was a pandemic that helped *Little Buckingham* finally reach completion and appreciation.

I'm most proud of the effect of center depth in the tubular flowers, as it appears as though you could put your finger well into the centers. I've learned a couple things throughout this long process, which I pass on to my students. One valuable lesson is when looking at a floral design, make sure the images are attached and not floating in space; flowers need a stem leading them back to ground.

**Patty Piek-Groth**
Janesville, Wisconsin

*Patty Piek-Groth has been hooking for 40 years and enjoys all styles of hooking and dyeing wool. She is a retired public-school teacher and is a McGown Certified Instructor. She is the assistant director of the North Central McGown Teachers Workshop.*

**In The Judges' Eyes:** *Color choices are pleasing. Shading is first rate. Good variety of greens, lovely.*

**Little Buckingham**, 24″ x 36″, #3- and 4-cut hand-dyed wool on burlap.
Designed by Jane McGown Flynn and hooked by Patty Piek-Groth, Janesville, Wisconsin, 2020.

# Marti's Fantasy

I first saw this piece in 2015 when it was still in its conceptual stage. I have always enjoyed crewel needlework, so I was drawn to *Marti's Fantasy*. I love the free-flowing motion and whimsical appearance of this piece—along with the animals, which attracted me to it immediately.

The owl, the quail, and the rabbit are my favorites. I hooked them realistically to set them apart from the fanciful flowers, motifs, and other elements of the rug.

When I first started to hook rugs, I was hooking primitives with a #6-cut strip. From there I "graduated" to a #3-cut strip. I enjoy fine shading—watching each and every element come to life as they do in a fine-cut, realistic rug. I've learned to balance my colors throughout the rug. Balancing colors and fine shading are crucial in this kind of rug.

**Tamzen Mackeown**
Middle Haddam, Connecticut

*Tamzen Mackeown first started to hook rugs in 2014, when she duplicated a rug her grandmother had hooked for her father, a World War II veteran. From there, with a rug hooking book for beginners in hand, she was self-taught until she found a weekly rug hooking group that encouraged her to take lessons. She has hooked both primitive and fine-shaded rugs.*

**In The Judges' Eyes:** *Beautiful shading to make each feature stand out. Well-hooked background. Lovely crewel colors.*

**Marti's Fantasy**, 38″ x 46″, #3-cut hand-dyed wool on monk's cloth.
Designed by Marti Rotchford and hooked by Tamzen Mackeown, Middle Haddam, Connecticut, 2021.

# Miss Wiegle

**Miss Wiegle**, 72″ x 26″, #6- and 8-cut hand-dyed wool on linen.
Designed by Gene Shepherd and hooked by Betty Allen, Norman, Oklahoma, 2021.

### Betty Allen
Norman, Oklahoma

*Betty Allen is 73 years old and she started hooking eight years ago. After her husband passed away, she ventured into rug hooking and it has been a great comfort in her life. She was a quilter for many years and she weaves, but rug hooking is her passion.*

**In The Judges' Eyes:** *The color placement is well balanced. Hooking is crisp, which makes each of the designs stand out. Beautiful bright colors add to this contemporary design.*

I had admired this rug for quite some time but I felt like it would be too difficult for me. It is geometric, and I find hooking geometric designs challenging. But I wanted to hook something where I was forced to go outside my comfort zone. So I decided to hook this smaller version of *Miss Wiegle*.

I was especially dreading the Greek key designs as well as the border on the ends. I was surprised that I really enjoyed hooking the Greek keys once I learned the technique. It was much easier than I expected and became a joy to hook.

I learned a lot about color as I worked on this rug. I knew I wanted black-and-white check and black for the background (although the black has lots of green and blue-black). My biggest obstacle was to color plan beyond that point. It took several days to figure out what was pleasing to my eye. The colors I originally planned did not work—all those small sections bumping up against each other made it difficult to settle on a color plan that did work. It is a very busy rug.

# *More Masks*

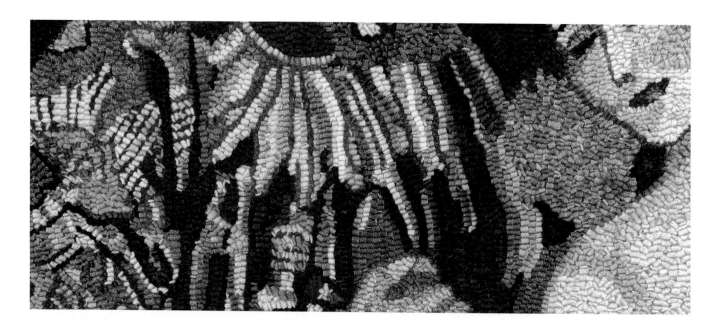

This is an adaptation of artwork by W. T. Benda (1873-1948), who was a painter, illustrator, and an accomplished theater mask and costume designer for stage productions in New York and London. I've long been tempted to hook some of his illustrations that appeared as magazine covers in the 1920s. This illustration was on the cover of *Theatre* magazine in 1921 and again on *Life* magazine in 1923. I decided to hook it as a nod to the reopening of theater in New York in the fall of 2021.

I love the drama of the piece; I think it evokes a lot of emotion. I saw various pictures of this illustration, and all were somewhat different in coloration—some were vibrant and some were faded. The actual vintage magazine covers are 100 years old now! So, while trying to stay true to the colors used by the artist, a lot was left open to interpretation. The wool for the woman's costume and mask I fused with tissue lamé fabric in four different colors, from gold to bronze.

Since this is an art-deco period piece, and given the style and color of her costume in the illustration, I imagined that in real life her costume would have been made in a lamé fabric. To achieve

that I used a fusing technique I learned in a class with Cindy Irwin a few years ago, which allows you to hook with materials that may be too delicate to hook with as is. The lamé fused wool was difficult to hook. I would not recommend hooking a large area in this way. It is a technique better suited for use in a small accent area.

I was particularly pleased with how the man's costume turned out. It was detailed and complicated, and I wasn't sure I could do the mask and robe justice. The robe was of most concern to me, especially the way it is detailed and clear close up, then fades and blurs a in the background. Add in the folds and shadows, and I was skeptical that it would translate well enough via hooking. The elaborate mask was also very detailed; I needed to use #2 cuts of wool for outlining, so mainly that just required a lot of patience!

Overall, I would not recommend hooking a large area in this way either. This too is a technique better suited for use in a small accent area. I knew that going into it, but for my purposes, it came out close to what I had envisioned, so I persevered with it.

I framed the rug in an era-appropriate frame.

### Jane Anderson
Clinton, New Jersey

*Jane Anderson is a wife, mother, retired marketing director, and an avid rug hooker since 2015. She is a member of the Hunterdon County Rug Artisans Guild in New Jersey.*

**In The Judges' Eyes:** *Stunning colors, expertly shaded. Very pleasing interpretation. Contrast in methods and materials between the two figures very well done.*

**More Masks**, 28″x 30″, #2- to 6-cut hand-dyed wool, tissue lamé fabric adhered to wool, and as-is wool on linen.
Designed by Wladyslaw T. Benda and hooked by Jane Anderson, Clinton, New Jersey, 2021.

# *Noel*

I hooked *Noel* with wool from my stash. It was fun remembering in which rug each wool was used. The red was mainly from my dummy board for Joan Moshimer's *Here Comes Santa!*. I had to use various reds from other projects to complete the bow. It was a challenge for me to get the reds blended correctly.

I would say I'm a traditional fine-cut hooker. I seldom use embellishments or materials other than dyed wool; I hook in a #3 or #4 cut.

I bound *Noel* with yarn left from dog sweaters I had knit for fund-raising benefits. That yarn was a perfect match to a shade in the bow. I covered the back with leftover fabric, then I had to decide how to hang it. I sewed tape to the top of the piece and purchased a small dowel and decorative end caps. I painted these gold. I tried to use the binding yarn to hang the piece, but it was not bold enough, so I got some trim from the fabric store.

In the late 1970s a friend asked me if I wanted to try rug hooking. We had done lots of arts-and-crafts things over the years, but this was really the first endeavor that required a teacher. We joined Yvonne Miller's class and learned everything from beginning to end. She is the only teacher I've ever had who insisted that I dye my own wool. I finished a strawberry chair pad and nearly finished Joan Moshimer's *Chinese Oriental* when my job forced me to put my hooking aside.

Long before I was introduced to hooking, I did knitting, cross-stitch, needlepoint, embroidery, and crewel work. Now when I'm not hooking, I knit socks and neckwear for all family members for Christmas gifts, and I knit various pieces for charity. I'm retired now.

### Sally Raub
**Lancaster, Pennsylvania**

*Sally Raub began hooking in the late 1970s but soon put hooking aside to work full time. In the 1990s she moved into a home down the street from Peggy Hannum and was delighted to learn that Peggy taught rug hooking. Her style fit nicely with what Sally had learned from her first teacher.*

**In The Judges' Eyes:** *Beautiful, rich holiday colors. Well shaded and finished expertly. A Christmas classic.*

**Noel**, 10″ x 33″, #3-cut hand-dyed wool on linen.
Designed by Pearl McGown and Jane McGown Flynn and hooked by Sally Raub, Lancaster, Pennsylvania, 2021.

# Persian Magic

I hooked this lovely Oriental design in colors to match other rugs in my home. With the incredible eyes of Betty McClentic, we picked the appropriate colors which I dyed with PRO Chem and Cushing dyes. The collaboration continued through the pandemic by email, deciding each motif as we went and assessing the successes (and making some changes) along the way. The homebound pandemic days passed quickly as the hooking gave me an outlet; I woke up each morning eager to hook.

The center was the most fun to hook, as there is a lot going on. The center of the rug is very graceful, with the arching fronds leading to the white flowers. It is busy but clean because of the colors.

The borders flowed easily, once they were set up. I dyed the whipping yarn to match the darkest blue and whipped a smaller-than-my-normal edge by cutting the backing and folding it forward.

A large background can be boring, so by mixing three and four values of red wool, I was more involved with the hooking; the viewer is as well, seeing more dimension. Hidden in the background movement is the year, my name, and some other words.

After steaming and steaming and steaming again, the backing was cut 1″ from the edge of the hooking. The edge was then turned upward twice and basted with whipping yarn dyed to match the darkest blue. I whipped the edge.

And then it was steamed twice again!

**Martha Beals**
Oakland, Maine

*A love of color and a desire to create rugs have given Martha Beals a wonderful life with hooked rugs. She is a retailer turned artist, teacher, and dyer.*

**In The Judges' Eyes:** *Superb color plan, extremely well executed. Beautiful interpretation and a pleasure to look at. Wonderful, variegated field.*

**Persian Magic**, 72″ x 96″, #3-, 4-, and 5-cut hand-dyed wool on monk's cloth.
Designed by Pearl K. McGown and hooked by Martha Beals, Oakland, Maine, 2021.

# Rebecca

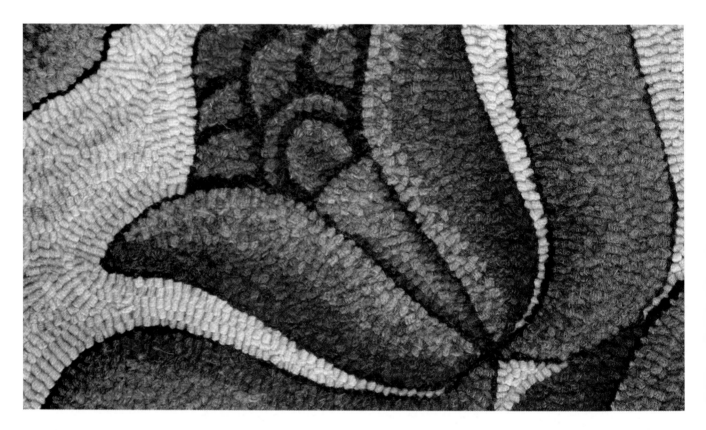

I really love the balance of this design created by Bea Brock. She traditionally hooks her rugs in gorgeous, bright colors, and I was inspired to put a twist on that by hooking it in muted colors. I was drawn to the pattern because of the balance and design. I really love how the center medallion draws the eye into the rug and then allows the eye to move around the entire rug.

I had a lot of fun color planning it, using a color palette I use in my decorating. The secondary purpose of the color palette I chose was to provide a nod towards primitive design. I added the twist of different values, which I felt the pattern lent itself to.

I thought the rug needed a border to balance the design and tie it together. While this was not overly challenging, I had to decide

where to place the line of the border. I ended up placing it under the leaves and other motifs to make the border even more subtle. I then used the same dye recipe I used in the center background and doubled it in strength to create the outside border color.

While color planning, I introduced the "poison" color of chartreuse, sparingly used in the color palette in the cording around the rug. I really love how this bright green plays with the deep red-purple color it lies against. How fun it was to add a "poison" color of a bright chartreuse into the muted mix! I was nervous about using it. But when I saw how exciting it was to have the green popping up in the muted colors, I fell in love.

**Mary McGrath**
Mukwonago, Wisconsin

*Mary McGrath has been hooking rugs since 2002. She loves working in values and fine cuts.*

**In The Judges' Eyes:** *Lovely soft colors. Well-shaded and well executed. Masterfully done.*

**Rebecca**, 45″ x 60″, #4-cut wool on linen.
Designed by Bea Brock and hooked by Mary McGrath, Mukwonago, Wisconsin, 2021.

# *Sahand*

This is the only rug design made by my close friend Jane Olson that I have ever hooked, so it has become a tribute/memory rug for me. Once I saw Jane's traditional design, I immediately determined to interpret it in a very non-traditional way—using wide cuts, highly-mottled odd scrap wool, very little outlining, and antigodlin hooking.

Although traditional Persians tend to be made with a few different solid colors, I opted to use many members of a color family, in both solids and textures, to fill the various sections of the rug. That choice, coupled with wider cuts, brought a lot more interest and drama to the design. I think it causes the viewers' eyes to move more around the rug. It also fits my usual scrappy approach to hooking.

The center and corner medallions were what drew me to this rug. And I did immediately start in the center when I started hooking because I loved the interplay of similar colors that were used to fill the various color sections. It has an opulent old look that I like very much.

When I was halfway through the center medallion, I realized the pattern had slipped during drawing, so much so that three of the corner medallions were off-grid by as much as 1 to 1½". To correct this required a total redraw as well as some center medallion tweaking. It also made for a very messy and confusing pattern. Had it not been one of my friend's last patterns, I doubt I would have continued.

The large spaces of blank background around the medallions ended up being quite troublesome to me—probably because most old Persians have very busy backgrounds. After playing around with various approaches, I determined that I did not like the blankness—or any of the design additions I could come up with to put in that space. Eventually, I upped my dark-red background color options from just five or six choices, adding another five or six choices in various orange-red hues. This gave me a broad enough palette to "fill" the blank void with much more interesting color.

The main lesson from hooking this rug? Before you start, make sure the design is square to the fabric. If it isn't, don't hook it.

Despite all the trouble this rug caused me, it has turned out to be one of my favorite hooked pieces. I think that is because I loved Jane Olson.

**Gene Shepherd**
Anaheim, California

*Gene Shepherd began hooking in 1998. He started teaching and writing about rug hooking in 2000 and began making instructional videos in 2005.*

**In The Judges' Eyes:** *Wow, a real showstopper. Brilliant colors make this a stunning rug. Color plan is well done, as is the hooking and finishing.*

**Sahand**, 31″ x 49½″, #6- and 8-cut hand-dyed wool on monk's cloth.
Designed by Jane Olson and hooked by Gene Shepherd, Anaheim, California, 2020.

# Southern Pines

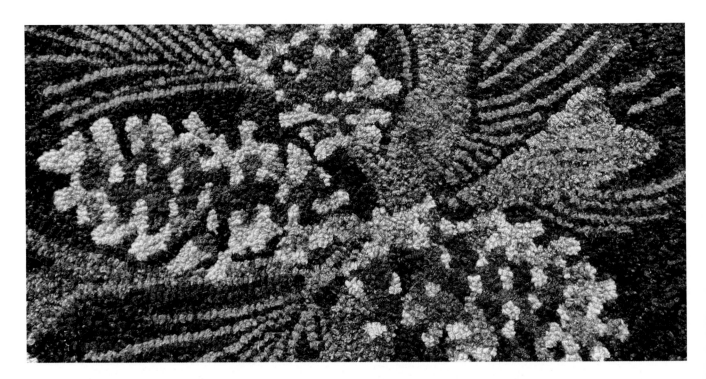

I had no idea how I was going to hook this piece or even if I wanted to—there are a lot of pinecones in this design! My rug hooking friends Judy Carter and Margaret Wenger met me at a local shop that was going out of business, and we color planned the rug from what wool was left on the shelves. The rug is hooked with "as-is" wool. I think choosing the undyed wool makes it more natural and realistic.

The background is my favorite part of the rug. The multi-colored plaid brought all the colors together and really set off the pinecones. I didn't need to blend anything—it just happened on its own. Most of the comments I get on this rug are about the background. It's amazing how one piece of wool can make a rug successful.

The scales of the pinecones were the most challenging. I had to make sure they didn't blend together. Since I only had a few different wools to work with, to make it easier I started at the top of each cone and hooked each scale completely, then hooked the scales on either side of the first one. Also, the outside scales needed to be light enough that they didn't get lost in the background.

This is a big rug—I should have had more than a lap frame to make it easier to handle. It took me 10 years to finish this rug—and many months passed in between hooking, so keeping good notes was critical. On a rug this size, I recommend that you hook the motifs and background as you go. Also, be certain that you have enough material for your project before you begin. I bought all the background wool that was available, not knowing if it would be enough.

**Cyndi Fisher**
Wyomissing, Pennsylvania

*Cyndi Fisher has been rug hooking for almost 20 years. She loved looking at antique rugs at auctions and wanted to learn how they were made, so she started taking classes from local teachers. Some of her projects are from vacation photographs.*

**In The Judges' Eyes:** *Harmonious use of colors. Background works so well with the pines. Beautiful in its simplicity. Color plan is well done, as is the hooking and finishing.*

**Southern Pines**, 47″ x 69″ #3-, 4-, 6-, and 8-cut wool on linen.
Designed by Pearl K. McGown and hooked by Cyndi Fisher, Wyomissing, Pennsylvania, 2021.

# Sunset

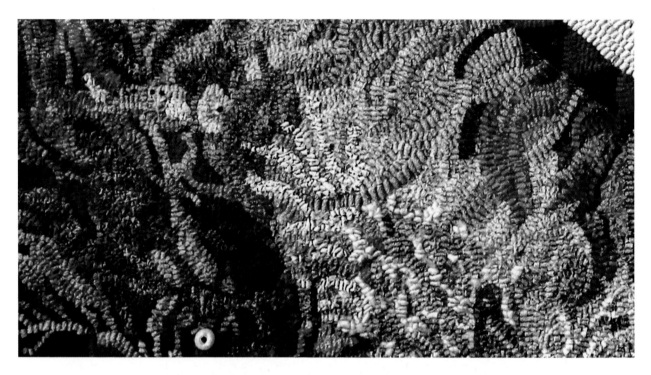

A friend asked me to hook this rug. She had started the project in a workshop but decided not to complete it. I was delighted to hook the pattern, although the prospect was a bit daunting! My friend gave me all the wool that her teacher had dyed for the project, and I used some wool from my stash as well. In addition, I incorporated hand-dyed silk, ribbon, tiny beads, and antique buttons into the piece to add interest and detail to the marine plants and animals.

I love the crab with his large button eyes, which are meant to look like eyes on stalks. I'm also fond of the squid and the seahorse. I embellished the body of the seahorse with dozens of tiny, pale-blue seed beads.

There were no swatches or dip dyes in the wool I had, so shading was difficult. I solved that problem by using color and value to achieve contouring, such as in the eyelids and areas

below the eyes. The other difficult area was making the black-and-red border around the sun perfectly even. It was a tedious process, which involved constantly counting the rows of loops, but the result was satisfactory.

I wanted the rug to have a minimalist appearance with no border. I folded the excess linen to the back and sewed brown cotton binding tape close to the last row of hooking. After trimming the excess linen, I tacked down the tape on the reverse to give a smooth, finished look.

This was one of the most difficult projects I have ever tackled. I have tremendous admiration and respect for the artist, David Galchutt, now that I have tried to copy his elaborate composition and subtly reproduce that in wool.

### Helen Mar Parkin
Lindale, Texas

*Helen Mar Parkin is a retired conservator of paintings who discovered rug hooking in retirement in 2011. She is a McGown Certified Instructor and a member of ATHA.*

**In The Judges' Eyes:** *Wonderful interpretation, well done. Beautiful bright colors add to this contemporary design. All elements well represented, lots of detail.*

CASEY SQUYRES

**Sunset**, 24½″ x 32¼″, #3- to 6-cut hand-dyed wool, sari silk, and ribbon on rug warp, embellished with old buttons and beads. Designed by David Galchutt and hooked by Helen Mar Parkin, Lindale, Texas, 2020.

# The Fruits of the Earth

This pattern was started at a Teacher Trainee Workshop over 20 years ago. It was never finished. I finally decided to finish it during repairs to my house from hurricane damage. The #3 cut kept my mind occupied from depressing thoughts.

As I worked on this rug, I became attached to this girl—I even talked to her. She kept me busy and kept me company through a rough time.

I was trained on #3 cut many years back. At that time, we only had patterns printed on burlap backing. The burlap was in good condition, even after 20 years, so I just kept hooking on it. The pattern had been started using wool swatches, which give the most detail and help with shading. Using swatches enhanced the detailing throughout.

I like that bowl full of fruit. Normally, I do not like hooking fruit, but this time the fruit hooked up easily. I used swatches to give the detail and shading. Shading on the face, throat, chest,

and hair were the most challenging parts. I worked a bit at a time on each area, and I used the "squint your eyes" method a lot to see if anything stood out or was glaringly out of place.

I finished the rug by mounting it on foam core. I pinned the burlap backing to the edges of the foam core, then I pinned a solid piece of dark-blue wool to this and whipped it over the back of the board to cover the edges.

Patience, patience, and more patience. I learned to have patience while working on this rug. My training with #3 cuts paid off on this rug. This pattern was one of the hardest and most involved rugs I have worked on in a long time. The pattern looked easy until I had to match up swatches.

My mother, Ruby Turnbull, started hooking back in the 1970s. She encouraged me to take one of the courses she taught at the local university and started me hooking a rose pattern. I still have the pillow I made from that piece.

**Amzi Collins**
Lake Charles, Louisiana

*Amzi Collins has been hooking rugs since 1983, when she learned from her mother, Ruby Turnbull. Amzi is a McGown Certified Instructor who teaches in her home and repairs old hand-hooked rugs. She believes that rug hookers should learn all that they can from the older generation and then pass it along to the younger generation.*

**In The Judges' Eyes:** *Nicely shaded. Well framed. Great expression on the woman's face.*

**The Fruits of the Earth**, 22″x 36″, #3-cut wool on burlap.
Designed by Jane McGown Flynn and hooked by Amzi Collins, Lake Charles, Louisiana, 2021.

# Tulay

I hooked *Istanbul*, by Jane McGown Flynn, and I loved the variety of motifs in that rug, so it seemed only natural for me to hook the companion rug, *Tulay*. Nancy Blood color planned each of these rugs so they would go together but not be the same color plan. The colors are electric in both rugs, and I loved hooking the peacocks.

I hooked *Tulay* on monk's cloth, which is always my backing of choice. The monk's cloth allows me to split the fibers to give the motifs more definition. I used a very bright ombre wool for the feathers that come out from the eyespot. This wool is difficult to hook in a #3 cut; however, it was ideal for the dramatic look of the peacock's train feathers.

I loved everything about hooking the peacocks. The colors are almost iridescent when I dye the formulas over chartreuse, Christmas green, and turquoise wool. I loved dyeing the variety of colors in the peacock eyes and surrounding them with the feathers, hooked with the bright ombre wool. This made them vibrant and alive.

Since the peacock was such an important part of the rug, I wanted the feathers to be as bright as those of a real peacock. The peacock eyespots are beautiful shades of salmon and brilliant blue. Surrounding the eyespots are delicate, wispy feathers. The bright ombre was the perfect group of colors to compli-

ment the eyespot, but the fabric easily fell apart when it was cut into a #3-cut size. Instead, it had to be torn on the weft of the weave—thus the challenge. When hooking the delicate feathers, I put in a placeholder of white wool. When I had finished hooking the feathers, I removed the placeholder and hooked the ombre in the holes. This made all the difference, and I think it makes the peacock come alive.

The background is a spot dye from *Nancy's Color Beauties Book 1* called Plum Duff. This is a very deep eggplant color, and I could not find any yarn to match this. I finally ended up using the background fabric cut in a #3 cut to attach the binding tape. It was really difficult, but the end result is just what I wanted. I sewed the other side of the binding tape to the rug.

When I was beginning to hook years ago, I was subscribed to "Rug Hooking News and Views." I called Joan Moshimer to ask her if she knew of any teachers in my area. She said I was lucky because one of the best teachers lived nearby. Margaret Howell took me into her afternoon class with a group of older women who had been meeting together for many years. They became like second mothers to me and were just what I needed as I was so far from home. I realize now how very lucky I was to have had her as my mentor until 1980, when we moved to Oklahoma. She taught me so much, and I still miss her.

**Lee Williams**
Stigler, Oklahoma

*Lee Williams started hooking in 1970 in New York. When she moved to South Carolina she began fine-cut hooking with Margaret Howell. She left there in 1980 and she stopped hooking until 2016, when she began again. She loves all fiber arts.*

**In The Judges' Eyes:** *The yellows hold up very well without overpowering the rug. Well done! Lively colors and beautiful shading make this a superior work of art.*

**Tulay**, 44″ x 78″, #3-cut hand-dyed wool on monk's cloth.
Designed by Jane McGown Flynn and hooked by Lee Williams, Stigler, Oklahoma, 2020.

# White Doves and Peonies

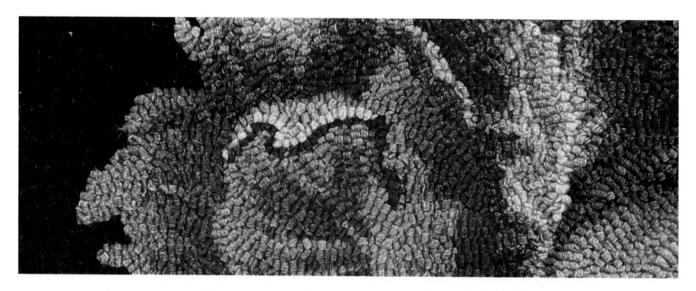

I originally selected this pattern for a fine-cut shading class to be held in Canada in May 2020. I was drawn to the flowers on the pattern and felt they would be perfect for the class. Planning to attend with my friend and local teacher, Linda Powell, we were both disappointed when the class was cancelled due to the pandemic. We wanted to continue with the project, so Linda and I started to prepare via phone, Zoom, and "no contact" porch drop-offs. Eventually we were able to meet in person.

The original class was to be a fine-cut shading course, so Linda suggested dyeing methods that would teach me how to shade using a variety of techniques. I used short, 3- and 5-inch dyed pieces with a gradation from light to dark on the cherry blossoms and the blossom leaves. Linda referred to this type of dyeing as "sausage dyed." Different lengths of dip-dyed pieces were used for the peony petals and the peony leaves. The doves were hooked using valued swatches, and the rock and moss were hooked with subtle spot-dyed and mottled wools.

The sausage- and dip-dyed pieces were wonderful to work with and made a smooth transition from light to dark without continually hooking a few loops and cutting (as when working with valued swatches).

The peonies are my favorite because of the three-dimensional result I was able to achieve. The doves were challenging because I needed to achieve a separation between the two. The detail in the wings was also a challenge. I made one dove a bit darker and reverse-hooked the wings until I achieved the look I wanted.

This was a good study in shading, and I learned how to achieve depth and dimension by using and manipulating these different dyed wools.

My husband and I were celebrating an anniversary in historic Zoar, Ohio. The bed and breakfast had hand-hooked rugs throughout the house, and I knew I wanted to learn more. Before I left, the owner furnished me with a kit to get started on my own. Then I pursued local teachers and groups in my area.

These days I crochet and do some wool appliqué, but mostly I hook rugs. However, I like to learn new techniques and have taken classes in needle felting and punch needle.

**Norita Blue**
Norton, Ohio

*Norita Blue began hooking rugs eight years ago and she has taken many classes and tried many techniques. She enjoys learning and continues to develop new methods. Her favorite projects are pictorials.*

**In The Judges' Eyes:** *Oriental feel to the colors in this piece, vibrant. Beautiful shading and vivid colors combine with a dark-blue background make a pleasant harmonious scene. Lovely bright peonies.*

**White Doves and Peonies**, 20″ x 36″, #3-cut hand-dyed wool on linen.
Designed by Jane McGown Flynn and hooked by Norita Blue, Norton, Ohio, 2021.

# A Study in Portraiture

Retirement—time to travel and time to join a rug hooking group. I immediately did both; joined a group and hooked with them bi-weekly for a few months and then headed off to Madeira for a month. I got home just in time for COVID-19 to tie me to the house.

Oh, well. That meant I had more time. And not being able to travel, it meant more time to hook—hook on my own and hook with others via Zoom. That first year of COVID-19 meant all my unfinished projects got completed. And then came year two.

More time to hook! Time to take advantage of one of the many on-line courses available. Time I could really challenge myself to see how far I could push my rug hooking skills. A great opportunity soon made itself available. Liz Marino offered a course on hooking portraits. Expecting to learn a lot, but not being too optimistic of my ability to put those learnings into practice, I eagerly signed up.

The first step was to find a portrait by an artist who had been dead for a century or more to eliminate any copyright issues. My choice was the *Portrait of Delphine Ingres-Ramel* by the French neoclassical artist Jean-Auguste-Dominique Ingres. This

portrait of his wife was completed by Ingres in 1859 and was the final portrait he painted. Ingres died in 1867, so this picture met the copyright criteria.

The focus of this rug is on the face and hand. After some false starts and lots of support from Liz, I finally curated the correct wool swatches for the skin tones and developed a feel for how to hook the face. I had imagined that the eyes would be the most difficult—how wrong I was. But I did discover that sleep was one of my best tools for this piece. I would spend hours over many days staring at the piece, trying to figure out the next step, and then discover the answer in my dreams!

As one of the final touches to the piece, I decided to incorporate my newly-learned bead-working skills into the portrait. I chose small beads that would lie flat with the hooking. I also made sure there was shading in the beadwork.

I found that the strategy for IT projects works for rug hooking as well. If you can break your piece into smaller sections and focus on one section at a time, you can hook almost anything. This project reminded me that rug hooking is not a race. Take the time you need to resolve the issues in each small section.

**Jennifer Curran**
Oakville, Ontario

*Jennifer Curran is retired from a career in Information Technology. A member and certified teacher of the Ontario Hooking Craft Guild, Jennifer is also a McGown Certified Instructor, and a member of the Guild of Pearl K. McGown Hookrafters and ATHA. COVID-19 has given her the opportunity to meet rug hookers from across Canada and the United States and to join the Woolwrights Rug Hooking Guild in Pennsylvania, in addition to her local rug hooking group in Etobicoke, Ontario.*

**In The Judges' Eyes:** *Effective border treatment. The colors and shading bring the face to life. The addition of the real jewelry adds a wonderful touch.*

**A Study in Portraiture**, 19½″ x 21″, #3-cut wool on linen.
Designed and hooked by Jennifer Curran, Oakville, Ontario, 2021.

# Clare Bridge Over the River Cam

I grew up in Suffolk, England, and moved to America when I was 15 years old. I returned to the very same area 25 years later, when my husband and I were stationed there with the US Air Force. We often traveled to Cambridge and loved walking the surrounding areas. I love the outdoors and I have walked along the River Cam many times. Although it does rain a lot in England, I can attest to the fact that they sometimes do have beautiful sunny days.

When I was looking to make a landscape rug, I came across this picture of the river Cam in Cambridge and knew instantly that this was to be my next project. What drew me to this photograph was the beautiful lighting.

My rug is 100% wool. Some of the wools are very textured to give realism to the foliage, stone, and water. I wanted the sky to contrast and seem peaceful, so I chose much softer, less-textured wool. My biggest challenges with this rug were making sure that it didn't look like a big green blob and making the water look real. Hopefully I was able to capture enough depth and highlights to define the elements and create movement on the water. Green is my favorite color, and I was able to capture so many shades between the trees and river.

Although this seemed like a good idea at the time, I soon realized that I enjoy hooking the most when I just do what comes naturally. It's important to do what you love—don't feel like you need to compare your work to anyone else's.

**Karen Misiewicz**
Plattsmouth, Nebraska

*Karen Misiewicz has loved creating things her whole life. From the time she was a child she has had some sort of project going. She loves trying new things but her favorite things are the fiber arts. She hooked her first rug hooking project from a little kit she purchased while in England.*

**In The Judges' Eyes:** *Excellent use of values to show detail. Lovely pictorial. Well done.*

**Clare Bridge Over the River Cam**, 35" x 24", #4- and #6-cut wool on linen.
Designed and hooked by Karen Misiewicz, Plattsmouth, Nebraska, 2021.

# *Fasnacht*

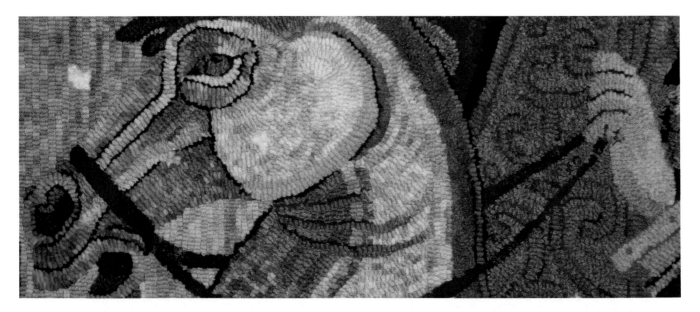

I chose this design for the 2021 Magic of Michele Micarelli and David Galchutt retreat at Sauder Village Rug Hooking Week. To create the pattern, I purchased the original painting from David and secured permission to make it into a rug pattern. I then sent a picture of *Fasnacht* to Michele for her help to color plan the piece.

Fasnacht, German for Fast Night, is celebrated on Shrove Tuesday, the Tuesday before Ash Wednesday (also known as Fat Tuesday). Fasnachts are doughnuts, often in the shape of a pretzel, made to help deplete the pantry of lard, butter, and sugar going into the Lenten season. Fasnacht Day is celebrated in Lancaster, Pennsylvania, where you can find some of the delicious fasnachts.

The wools are all hand dyed by Michele Micarelli and me. Michele's beautiful wools and colors helped bring the rug to life. The snowflakes and snow in the trees are hooked with white velvet.

There are two sections that I like the most: The face surrounded by the ruff collar and the brocade coat sleeve. I love the brocade pattern designed for the coat sleeve, but I am very pleased with the results of the Elizabethan ruff collar.

It took me a while to begin working on that collar. I studied the colors and folds in the original painting and began hooking a small section. Once I stepped back, I could see that what I completed was going to work for the rest of the collar.

The rug was finished using corded wool with integral facing made from Bay Harbour wool from Two Ewenique Sheep, and hand-sewn to the piece.

Attention to detail is paramount when working with a David Galchutt design. The original painting with all its intricate details is small—only 6½" x 9". The rug is 29" x 39", and it required a lot of effort to create a semblance of the original painting.

### Dennis Seyller
#### Chesapeake, Virginia

*Dennis Seyller is retired and living the good life. He began rug hooking at the 2006 ATHA Convention in New Orleans after many years of traveling with his wife, Susi, to various rug hooking events. He has many more rugs to hook and many ideas to develop.*

**In The Judges' Eyes:** *Great detail. Whimsical interpretation with excellent choice of color and shading. Very nice use of color palette and great interpretation of the subject.*

**Fasnacht**, 28″x 39″, #2- to 4-cut hand-dyed wool on rug warp. Designed by Dennis Seyller from a painting by David Galchutt (with permission), and hooked by Dennis Seyller, Chesapeake, Virginia, 2021.

JANINE HOBBS

# Firefly Memories of the Great Smoky Mountains National Park

I was inspired to hook this scene after seeing a photograph by Floris van Breugel in *The New York Times* of swarming fireflies in the Great Smoky Mountains National Park and by my memories of a childhood visit there.

I love working in wool. I like to use a lot of textures in my rugs. I have a significant stash of recycled woolens from wool clothing acquired from secondhand stores during visits to Michigan. I didn't discover places like Dorr Mill Store until I connected with other rug hookers.

I'm pleased with how the sky turned out. It is twilight and I wanted a hint of the sunset. It also gave all the shadows a coherent orientation. I used six shades of blue.

The green understory of the forest was challenging. I wanted to show the depth of the forest through color. I read a painting blog from Mary Gilkerson that gave me some good straightforward suggestions.

Making the edge of the piece with stepped corners was challenging. I had to figure out how to protect the linen from unraveling and not have too much thickness or excess linen. I stitched the inside "corner", used Fray Check on the cut edge of the linen, and finished the back with a piece of thick wool cut to cover the shape of the entire stepped corner.

For the final finish, I turned the linen to the back and whipped stitched along with the twill tape. The corners were done separately, with a piece of thick wool cut to match the step shape of the corners.

Two lessons from this rug: How to express depth in a landscape using a progression of color, and how to securely finish irregular edges.

I have a degree in Industrial Design. It was a degree in problem solving that I was able to extend to many of my endeavors.

I create the designs for my own rugs. This is my first adaption. My rugs all have a story to tell. I do research my topic once I settle on what I want to explore.

I ran out of background fabric on the rug I'm now working on. No hair was torn out or tears shed for my lack of skill calculating how much I needed. I simply found a similar fabric in my stash and dyed it to have a similar effect. Lots of taking out loops and replacing them, but I learned a good lesson: Better to have extra. I always do that when I cook!

**Deborah Kelman**
Foster City, California

*Retired from her catering business, Deborah Kelman learned rug hooking from books and the internet. She draws her own designs and dyes a lot of her wool. Rug hooking has helped her maintain a vestige of sanity.*

**In The Judges' Eyes:** *Interesting border and frame add creative touch. Well-designed and lovely color planned scene. Love the fireflies. Very nice use of color palette and great interpretation of the subject.*

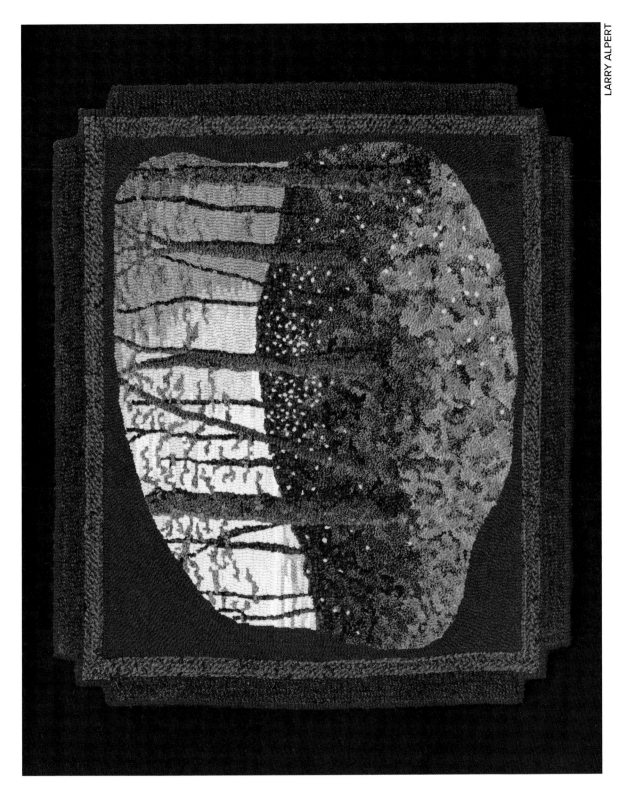

**Firefly Memories of the Great Smoky Mountains National Park,** 32½" x 27½", #4- to 8-cut hand-dyed and as-is wool, recycled wool, and hand-dyed yarn on linen. Designed and hooked by Deborah Kelman, Foster City, California, 2021.

# In the Sticks

My son, Will Arington, is a rancher near Anselmo, Nebraska. He annually competes in the Pitzer Ranch Horse Invitational in Ericson, Nebraska. The horse-and-rider teams run an obstacle course, including crossing a river at breakneck speed, loading a steer into a trailer while on horseback, dragging things, jumping things, and performing general duties that could be necessary in the life of a ranch horse. Then they sort bulls, team rope, heading and heeling, and finish off the day running a barrel race. The idea is to show the versatility of the quarter horses bred by the Pitzer Ranch, who all come from the great stallion Two Eyed Jack. There is much money to be won and, of course, great prestige for the winners.

It is all great fun to watch. The obstacle course offers the greatest opportunity for disaster. I chose this photo, taken by Clarissa Castor during the obstacle course, to adapt into my rug. The horse and rider must jump this intimidating pile of brush and sticks.

I have hooked many horses and cowboys and always think I have a great advantage because I know how all the gear hooks up. But how to make the pile of sticks look individual, yet collectively massive, was my challenge in this piece. I worked with the fabulous Diane Stoffel and used 40 different colors of wool to make it all work.

I always think "light, bright, dark, dull." Color is important, but that mantra is even more important.

My favorite part of the rug? I love that the palomino mare appears to be jumping right out of the rug. The greatest challenge? Sticks, sticks, so many sticks. I tackled them one 50-cent piece at a time. Please remind me to never hook sticks again.

But I learned that something as boring as a pile of sticks can be interesting and challenging to hook.

## Janice Lee
### Valley, Nebraska

*Janice Lee has been rug hooking for over 20 years and owns The Rug Hooking Store at Black Horse Antiques in Valley, Nebraska, specializing in hand-dyed wool and rug hooking supplies. She is a McGown Certified Instructor whose hobbies include horses and dog training and playing the French horn.*

**In The Judges' Eyes:** *Great color choice. Superior shading. Wonderful detail in foreground. Very nice use of color palette and great interpretation of the subject.*

**In the Sticks,** 32" x 22", #3-, 4-, and 5-cut wool on linen.
Designed and hooked by Janice Lee, Valley, Nebraska, 2020.

# Mommie's Little Helper

My inspiration was a photo my granddaughter took of her son, Misha, who loves to help his mom with her thesis for her doctoral degree in botany.

I used narrow strips to obtain detail in the rug. I dyed the flesh color with avocado; the background wool was penny dyed with pennies, ammonia, and water in a glass jar and put in the sun. The rest of the rug was hooked with leftover wool strips from other rugs.

Misha's hair is bleached from the Hawaiian sun, and the wool I had on hand was a little too dark to show the light color of the hair on top of his head. My friend gave me some golden-colored mohair yarn that she rescued from a sweater, and I worked it in with my wool to add the needed brightness.

I loved hooking Misha's chubby little baby face, arms, and legs. Shading his little fingers was easy, and I love the way they turned out. The most challenging thing about this rug was the simple flowerpot. I hooked it over several times, and it just doesn't look like I want it. I tried several different colors, but none worked. I am still not pleased with the way it looks.

To finish this rug I first zigzag-stitched around the outside of the rug (on the rug warp backing) about 2″ to 3″ inches away from the last row of loops. Then I cut the excess rug warp away and discarded it. I rolled the 3″ of rug warp under twice, pinned it, and then machine-zigzagged on top to hold it in place. The rug warp now measured about ½″.

Next, I cut my binding from washed wool fabric in strips 5″ wide from selvage to selvage. Then I turn the long edge of the fabric under about ½″ to 1″ and hand-stitch the folded edge to the rug as close to the loops as possible, starting part way up one side, NEVER on a corner. Don't bother making pleats or darts in the binding for the corners. Just simply ease the wool around the corner; don't stretch it or pull it tight. The wool will naturally turn up and over the binding and you will finish it on the back of the rug later. To join the ends of the binding wool, don't turn the short edge of the binding under. Just overlap it about 1½″ and hand-baste it with large basting stitches. After inspecting your stitching on the front of the rug, turn all the binding to the back of the rug, gently tugging the corners to the back and folding them neatly on the back. Stitch down with large stitches. Turn the rug to the front again and pin the binding down so the part you turned over the rug warp is even all around; hand-stitch it down through the whole binding (including front, rug warp, and the back wool). On the back of the rug, hand-stitch the excess wool down. No need to turn it under or hem it. Wool naturally lays down, and it will be fine.

It's so much fun to hook people, especially your loved ones, from photos. Shading Misha's arms and legs made him come alive and you can "feel" how soft they are.

**Marilyn Becker**
Wausau, Wisconsin

*Marilyn Becker has been hooking for seven years and enjoys hooking family portraits and pets. Hooking is the best therapy a person could have, it's soothing, and builds confidence. It also builds lasting and wonderful friendships.*

**In The Judges' Eyes:** *Great memory rug. Made me smile! Memory captured well.*

**Mommie's Little Helper**, 24″ x 33″, #2 to 4-cut wool and repurposed mohair yarn on rug warp.
Designed and hooked by Marilyn Becker, Wausau, Wisconsin, 2021.

# Missing Ewe

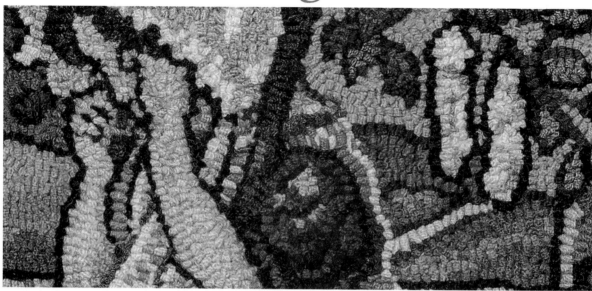

I have a passion for fairy tales and famous children's book illustrators. Many of my themed fairy tales and nursery rhyme rugs have been images from the late 1800s and early 1900s. This classic Little Bo Peep illustration by C. M. Burd (1873-1933) was a favorite of mine when I was a little girl. I've titled it *Missing Ewe* because of months and months of seclusion and social distancing due to COVID-19.

Back in the 1970s and '80s I worked for my father, who owned a punch/tuft hooking company called Rumpelstiltskins. I punched hundreds of rugs for our shops, catalogs, and demos. He advertised in *Rug Hooking* magazine back then, and I was mesmerized by the beautiful hooked rugs and dyed wool. Finally, in 2001, I attended Friends by the Sea camp in Rockaway, Oregon, to learn the traditional method. I loved it and my wonderful fellow hookers!

When COVID-19 started we canceled workshops, camps, and weekly gatherings and moved to Zoom. We decided to have a challenge rug theme, "Missing You," because, of course, we were really missing each other. Unfortunately, because the pandemic went on and on, we never went through with the challenge, but I hooked this little rug anyway.

I love the little lambs' faces. I think they make the piece less sorrowful, and they make me smile. Little Bo Peep's pinafore was portrayed as a small gingham print in the illustration, so I decided to use the beading method. The main difficulty was deciding where and how to put the folds, highlights, and shadows. I definitely used a bit of reverse hooking on that.

I loved the sentiment of the crying little girl and the humor of the lamb's tails hanging on the tree. Most of the colors were hand dyed except for the greens. I was able to use up many green as-is worms. Yay!

I'm looking forward to meeting and hooking together safely again soon.

**Katy Powell**
Milwaukie, Oregon

*Katy Powell has been a traditional rug hooker for over 20 years and before that she punched many rugs in the 1970s, '80s, and '90s. Her early years were spent in the performing arts, but now hooking has become her favorite artistic pastime. She loves the camaraderie and support of fellow hookers and the non-stressful focus time, alone at night after a long day of work.*

**In The Judges' Eyes:** *Pleasing bright colors. Beading technique on the dress is creative and clever. Wonderful rendition of a vintage illustration.*

**Missing Ewe**, 20″ x 20″, #3- and 4-cut hand-dyed and as-is wool on monk's cloth.
Designed by C. M. Burd and hooked by Katy Powell, Milwaukie, Oregon, 2020.

# Old French Fairy Tales

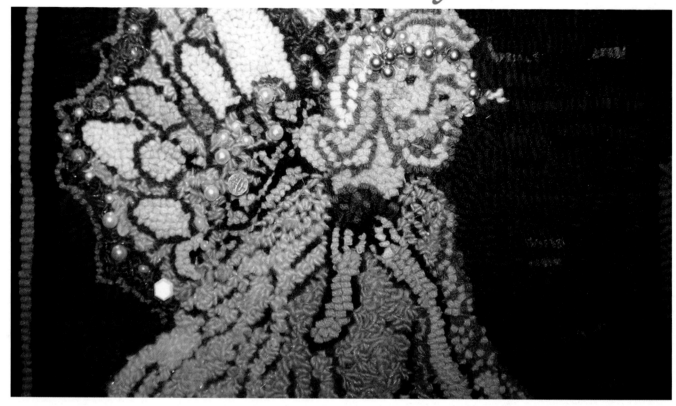

Artist Virginia Sterrett was born in Chicago, Illinois, in 1900. There, she enrolled in high school and later entered the Art Institute of Chicago on scholarship. One year after entering the institute, her mother grew ill and Sterrett dropped out to provide for her family. She gained work at an art advertisement agency. Sterrett received her first commission at the age of 19 (shortly after she was diagnosed with tuberculosis) from the Penn Publishing Company to illustrate *Old French Fairy Tales* (1920), a collection of works from the 19th-century French author, Comtesse de Ségur.

The artist created art-nouveau-style watercolors for this book. Her artwork is clean and exquisite, looking almost modern. I used #3-cut hand-dyed wool for the two figures and a #2 cut for the dark outline. The dress of the fairy is hooked with a fine wool yarn with silver highlights.

The fairy wings were most particularly challenging. As I was outlining with the thin black to fill in with light blue, I was apprehensive. But when I added the light-green wool yarn I had goose bumps. I knew I had achieved the ethereal look I was after.

Also challenging was the night sky. It was difficult to get the right hue. It was either too light or too dark. I removed my work several times until I finally got it right.

## Elyse Olson
### Fargo, North Dakota

*At age 17 at a Norwegian festival, Elyse Olson was awed and inspired by the intricate fine-cut hooked wool tapestries displayed from the local rug school. It was like walking into an art show—every tapestry was a masterpiece. The design, quality, and artistic expression were what motivated her to learn everything there was about rug hooking, and it is what drives her today, more than 30 years later.*

**In The Judges' Eyes:** *Great expressions on the two figures. Lovely colors. Wings are fabulous.*

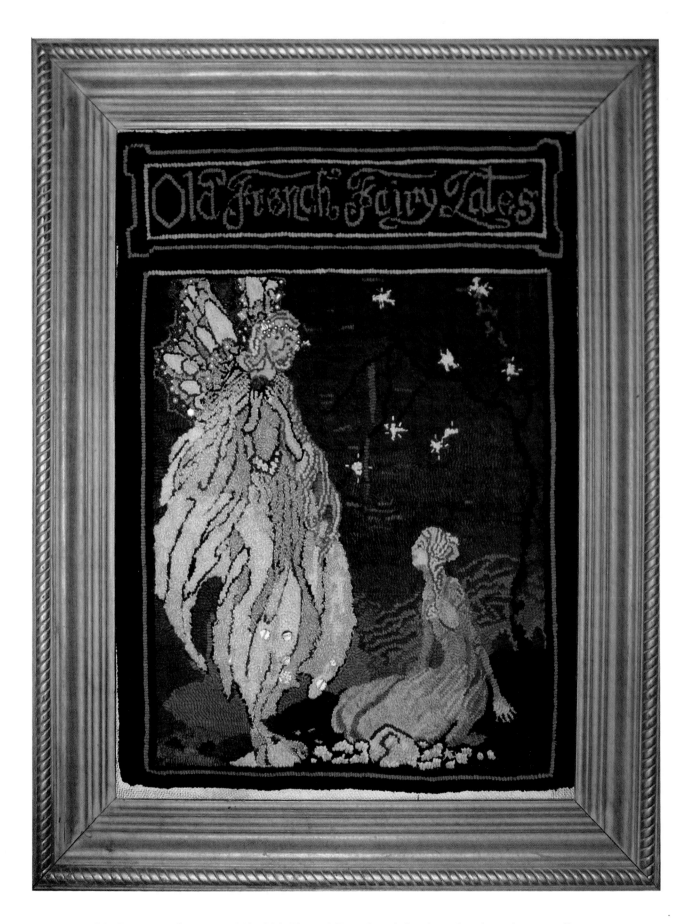

**Old French Fairy Tales**, 21″ x 29″, #3- and 5-cut hand-dyed wool and wool yarn on linen.
Designed and hooked by Elyse Olson, Fargo, North Dakota, 2021.

# Sentinel

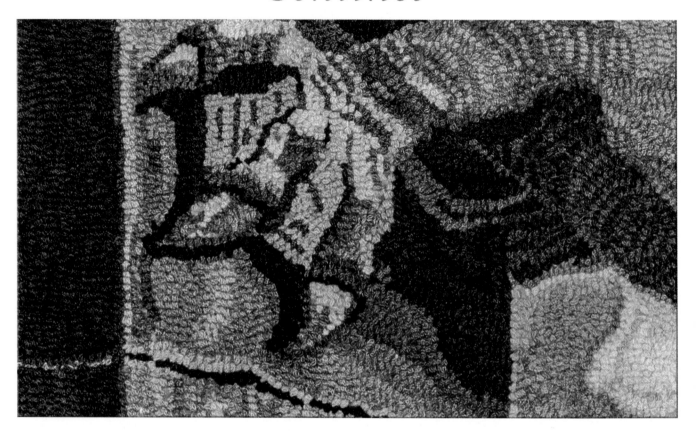

I fell in love with gargoyles when I was young and saw them on family vacations in New York City, Montreal, and Quebec. My father explained to me that gargoyles and grotesques were protectors of churches and other buildings and those people who inhabit them. Gargoyles also protect a building by spouting water away from buildings.

I continued to marvel at gargoyles when traveling home and abroad as an adult. I found a spectacular gargoyle image on a free image/royalty-free site. I had the image printed to the size I desired and used crack-stop to transfer the pattern to rug warp.

I used 100% wool in 16 values of gray and 12 values of taupe. I created the lightning by hand-spinning bright white wool, plied to a silver glitter novelty yarn, to hook into the sky. The guidance from teachers helped me as I hooked much of the rug when I stayed home to be cautious of COVID-19.

I love the eye because I felt two different storms were attacking her, along with the lightning. My gargoyle came alive with the glowering eye and is saying that she will protect at all costs. And I love the claw because she is holding onto what she has to defend at all costs.

This gargoyle represents my personal and professional life, as I have kept watch and am vigilant as I protect those I love. I am deeply grateful that rug hooking has become an integral part of my life.

**Katie O'Brien**
Duanesburg, New York

*Katie O'Brien has a PhD in Education Administration and Policy Studies and is a retired teacher and school administrator. She started rug hooking in 2015 and is a member of Loopy Ladies, Kinderhookers, Anne Arundel Rug Hookers, and ATHA.*

**In The Judges' Eyes:** *Marvelous use of colors to denote cold, blustery day. Wonderful menacing subject. Very expressive. A hugely successful piece.*

**Sentinel**, 25" x 19", #3-cut hand-dyed and hand-spun wool plied with novelty yarn on rug warp.
Designed and hooked by Katie O'Brien, Duanesburg, New York, 2021.

# Sunset Calling

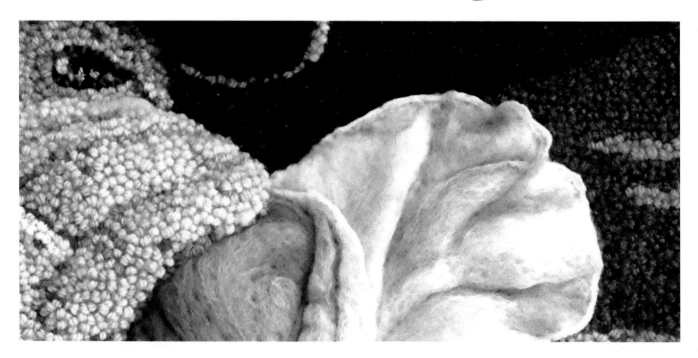

Upon moving to Maine full-time, I became good friends with my next-door neighbors, Donna and Les. Their property has several little cottages on it with knock-out ocean views. A tradition that they established long ago is for Les to play the conch shell while the sun is setting every summer night. Their daughter and son-in-law own a schooner named the Alert, and they make it a point to sail in front of the cottages for "sunset calling." It's an amazing experience that I'll never tire of.

Most of my art is hooked with wool yarn. Because I dye my yarn, it was easy to make the 23 shades of gray that were used for this piece. The border is hooked using a small houndstooth-patterned wool fabric. Making this a somewhat monochromatic rug, I wanted different depths of shades along with dimensional accents. I hooked the frame, background, Les's head and left hand fairly flat. The conch shell was felted with merino wool roving.

The span of gray shades creates lots of movement and interest. Creating the three layers almost makes this piece come alive. The shell was sewn onto the linen backing and stuffed, then the right hand was hooked separately and sewn over the shell for a more dimensional effect. A little sparkle was added with hooked embroidery thread for his two rings.

This was my first black-and-white hooked wall hanging, and it is a real favorite. It's especially nice when it brings to mind good memories about island living. There is no limit to hooking wall-hung rugs. I was a contemporary-quilting fiber artist for over 20 years and always wanted to try rug hooking. The first time that I hooked was a game changer and I never looked back.

**C. Susan Ferraro**
Bailey Island, Maine

*C. Susan Ferraro has been creating fiber art professionally for over 25 years. In her home state of Maine, she hooks rugs, and makes sculptures and wall hangings. Her original designs illustrate a combination of traditional rug hooking with unique dimensional features.*

**In The Judges' Eyes:** *Monochromatic shading is superior. Like everything about this rug! Man's expression, integration of conch shell, the border. Stunning! It all works so well together.*

**Sunset Calling**, 31″x 29″, Wool strips, hand-dyed yarn, needle-felted wool, and embroidery threads on cotton fabric. Designed and hooked by C. Susan Ferraro, Bailey Island, Maine, 2020.

# The Outhouse

When I saw my friend drawing her pattern I just had to get one. She drew me the pattern, and I got busy picking wool for the design while I figured out how to put a door on the outhouse. I hooked the inside of door first, then I added the door.

Just hook the door then cut around door about 1 inch. Place door on top of other door and hook the extra linen around the door and it turns out pretty nice.

**Karen Marker**
Annandale, Minnesota

*Karen Marker has been hooking about 17 years, with some long breaks in between. She loves wide cut strips and primitives. She finds hooking very rewarding.*

**In The Judges' Eyes:** *Fun piece, well executed. If this doesn't bring a smile to you, nothing will. Clever piece.*

**The Outhouse**, 27½″ x 30½″, #4-cut wool on linen.
Designed by Darlene Sjoberg and hooked by Karen Marker, Annandale, Minnesota, 2020.

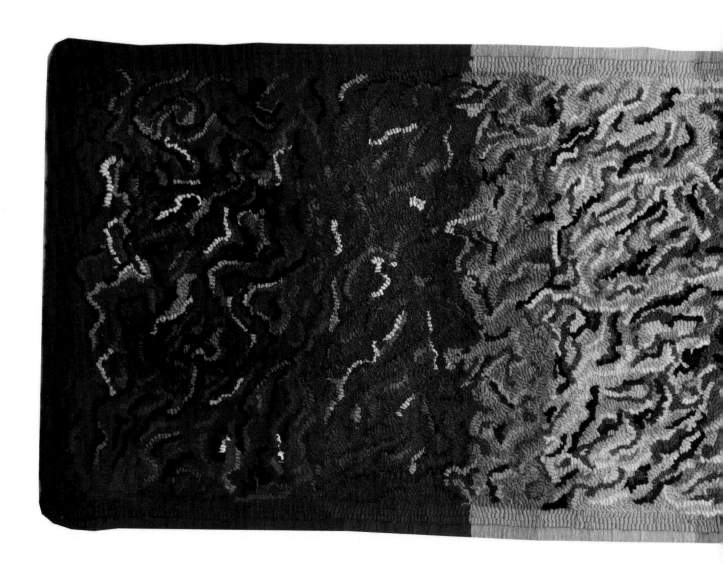

**Rainbow**, 47½″ x 17½″, #3- to 6-cut as-is wool on rug warp.
Designed and hooked by John L. Leonard, Wilmington, North Carolina, 2021.

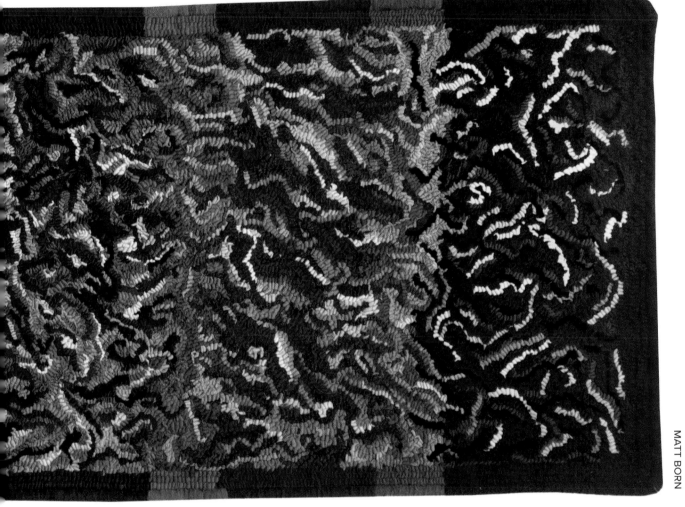

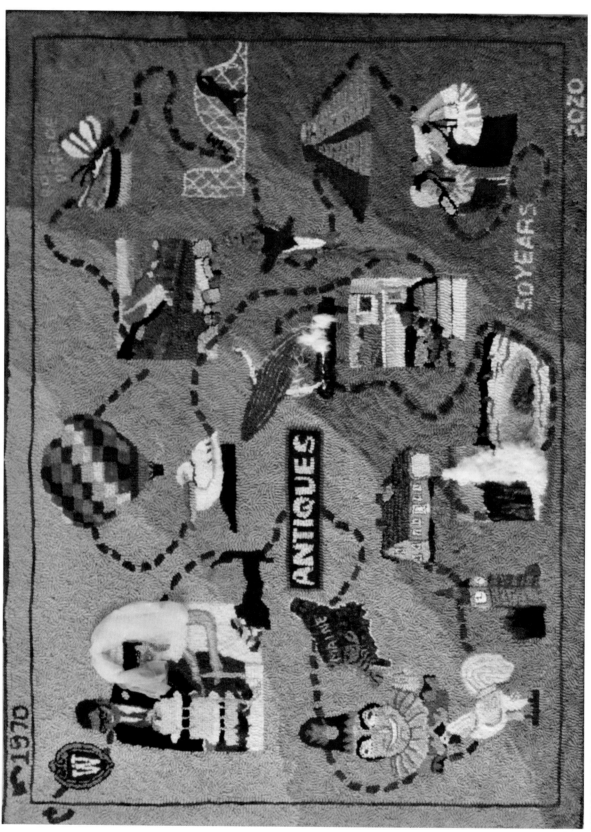

DENNIS DRIER

**50th Anniversary**, 41½″ x 31″, #3- to 6-cut hand-dyed and as-is wool and novelty yarns on monk's cloth.
Designed and hooked by Lyle Drier, Oconomowoc, Wisconsin, 2020.

**The Great Get Together Mask**, 70″ x 36″, disposable masks, reusable cotton masks, coffee filters, dryer sheets, elastic, hand wipes, rubber gloves, and fancy yarn on linen. Designed and hooked by Julie Hassler, Minneapolis, Minnesota, 2021.

JOSHUA FARR

**Cinnamon Ferns**, 23½" x 25", #6- to 8-cut hand-dyed and as-is wool on linen.
Designed and hooked by Suzanne Flynt, Dummerston, Vermont, 2021.

**Blue Goddess**, 25″ x 28″, #3- and 4-cut  hand-dyed and as-is wool and wool yarn on linen.
Adapted from a design by Diana Chelaru and hooked by Áine Humble, Halifax, Nova Scotia, 2021.

**Manarola, Cinque Terre, Italy,** 40½" x 18", #2- to 6-cut hand-dyed and as-is wool and wool yarn on linen. Designed and hooked by Arlette M. Spencer, Medicine Hat, Alberta, 2021.

**Angel**, 48" x 31½", #3-6-cut hand dyed wool on linen.
Designed by Christine Little of Encompassing Designs and hooked by Leisa Hillman, Valley, Nebraska, 2021.

DANIA ALBIN

**Peace Wall**, 37 ½" x 22", #8-cut hand-dyed and as-is wool on linen.
Designed by Rose Johnson and hooked by Debbie Abshier, Avon, Indiana, 2021.

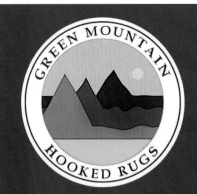
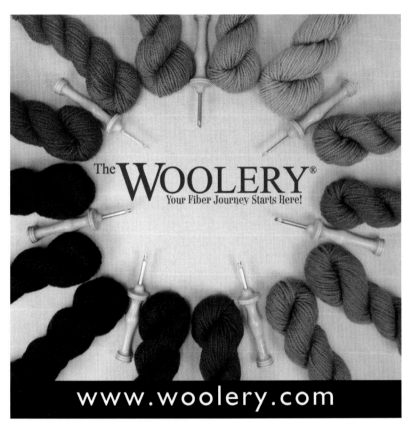
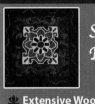

# Please Accept or Decline Your Book Club Benefits!

**Dear Rug Hooker,**

Please review the benefits of Book Club membership, and **join the *Rug Hooking* Book Club today!** We typically publish 4 books per year. And when you join now, we will send your **FIRST** book for an exclusive discount: only $9.95 USD, plus shipping and handling. That's HUGE savings for new Book Club members... more than 60% off the regular price! **Look at the benefits you'll receive:**

| | |
|---|---|
| ✓ **Guaranteed discounts on new books** | ✓ **Special sales only for book club members** |
| ✓ **Go green! Hassle-free automatic book payments** | ✓ **A free E-Newsletter with book club members-only content** |
| ✓ **Monthly discounts on our online store** | ✓ **First access to our newest books** |

## BONUS! Special one-time discount off your first book!

**RETAIL PRICE***

~~$28.95 USD~~

**BOOK CLUB PRICE***

~~$22.95 USD~~

**YOUR EXCLUSIVE PRICE**

**$9.95** USD

**To learn more about the *Rug Hooking* Book Club and become a Book Club Member today:**

 https://www.rughookingmagazine.com/RBC995

 (877) 297 - 0965 (U.S.) or (866) 375-8626 (Canada)

Exclusive offer for new Book Club members only!

*\*Retail and Book Club prices can vary with each title.*